FROM THE FILMS OF

Harry Potter

AFTERNOON TEA MAGIC

FROM THE FILMS OF

Harry Potter

AFTERNOON TEA MAGIC

OFFICIAL SNACKS, SIPS AND SWEETS
INSPIRED BY THE WIZARDING WORLD

INCLUDES CONTENT FROM

Text by Jody Revenson
Recipes by Veronica Hinke

CONTENTS

09 + INTRODUCTION

11 + CHAPTER ONE

SWEET FINGER TREATS AND SUGARY NIBBLES

13 + Hagrid's Pumpkin Teatime Madeleines

15 + Jacob Kowalski's Mini Teatime Paczki

18 + Hogwarts High Table Roasted Apple Scone Bites with Fresh Cream and Mint

20 + Divination Dream Bar Tea Treats

23 + Aunt Petunia's Teatime Windtorte Pudding

27 + Hungarian Horntail Mini Teatime Cakes

31 + Professor Umbridge's Load of Waffles

33 + Paris Pâtisserie Two-Bite Lavender Teatime Canelés

37 + Professor McGonagall's Transfigurational Sticky Toffee Pudding Bites

39 + Molly Weasley's Individual Teatime Rhubarb and Custard Trifles

42 + Professor Slughorn's One-Bite High Tea Profiteroles

45 + Kowalski Bakery's Occamy Egg Teatime Surprise

49 + Honeydukes Lemon Drop Meringue Teatime Bites

53 + One-Bite Circus Animal Tea Biscuits

57 + Queenie's Mini Brandied Apple Strudels with Apple Mint Sauce

60 + Professor Sprout's Bite-Sized Greenhouse Mystery Cakes

62 + Place Cachée Orange-Scented Teatime Pastry Puffs

65 + Hogwarts Houses Four-Layer Rainbow Petits Fours

67 + Dolores Umbridge's I Will Make Scones

68 + Teddy the Niffler's Two-Bite Gold Coin Sandwich Cakes

71 + Queenie Goldstein's Floating Teapot

75 + CHAPTER TWO:

SAVOURY TEATIME FINGER FOODS

77 + Durmstrang Institute Shopska Salad Tea Party Boats

79 + Mini Fried Raven Egg Tea Sandwiches

80 + Salade Niçoise Teatime Boat Bites

83 + Ron Weasley's Finger Sandwich Bites

85 + Leaky Cauldron Split Pea Teatime Soup

87 + Forbidden Forest Mini Mushroom Strudels

91 + Luna Lovegood's Honey-Roasted Radish Salad

92 + Black Lake Cod Cakes with Poached Eggs and Brandy Cream Sauce

95 + Deathly Hallows Pull-Apart Teatime Bread

97 + Great Hall Treacle and Pinot Noir–Roasted Turkey Drumsticks

101 + Bowtruckle Island Butter Board

102 + 'Good Gravy!' Mini Meat Loaf Tea Sandwiches

105 + Ron Weasley's Teatime Raspberry Jelly Treats

107 + Hagrid's Butternut Squash Mini Tartlets with Crispy Bacon and Sage

110 + Aunt Petunia's Teatime Ham Bites

112 + Tina Goldstein's Bite-Sized Hot Dogs with Honey Mustard Sauce

114 + Ron Weasley's Savoury Escargot-Stuffed Mushrooms

117 + Kowalski Bakery's Buttery Teatime Witch Hats with Magical Herbal Broomsticks

121 + Molly Weasley's Bangers and Roasted Tomato Quiche Bites

125 + CHAPTER THREE:

TEATIME SWEETS, SNACKS AND TAKE-HOME GIFTS

127 + Froggy Fancies

129 + Feverless Fudge Tea Bites

131 + Grandfather Goldstein's Teatime Owl Food

133 + Disenchantment Tea Jellies

135 + Pickled 'Ashwinder' Eggs

136 + Dementors Mini Chocolate Teatime Treats

139 + Chocolate Flying Keys

141 + Honeydukes Take-Home Lollipops

143 + Dumbledore's Elderberry Tea Pastilles

145 + CHAPTER FOUR:

TEATIME TIPPLES, HOT DRINKS AND MAGICAL MIXES

147 + Hogwarts House Teas

151 + Ginger Witch Whisky Sour

153 + Teddy the Niffler's Milk Treat

155 + Trevor's Toad Pond Punch

157 + Albus Dumbledore's Apple Butter and Brandy Hot Toddy

159 + Professor Trelawney's Divination Tea

160 + Goldstein Sisters' Cointreau Hot Chocolate

163 + The New York Ghost Wake-Up Call Drambuie Brew

165 + Professor Umbridge's Earl Grey Tea and Raspberry Champagne Cocktail

167 + Swooping Evil Blueberry and Mint Aviation Cocktail

169 + Professor Snape's Blueberry-Sage Spritzer

170 + DIETARY CONSIDERATIONS

171 + FRY STATION SAFETY TIPS

172 + METRIC CONVERSION CHART

174 + INDEX

INTRODUCTION

The Harry Potter films are quintessentially British, with an all-British cast at Hogwarts and Hogsmeade, all-British locations and even British Christmas crackers. In fact, through these films the Americans are learning about some of the British customs and are even beginning to pick up the British nomenclature: Ginny wears a jumper (sweater), Harry wears trainers (sneakers) and Luna Lovegood hopes there will be pudding (dessert) at the end-of-year feast.

In the Fantastic Beasts films, Englishman Newt Scamander travels to various cities on different continents. In Paris, his Niffler, Teddy, who has a penchant for shiny objects, liberates an important item from Gellert Grindelwald, which Newt passes to his friend and mentor, Albus Dumbledore, upon their return to Hogwarts. Dumbledore in turn offers the Niffler tea as a reward. (Newt suggests just milk instead and reminds Dumbledore to hide the teaspoons.)

Perhaps there is nothing more iconically British than an afternoon tea, served on a three-tiered china tray laden with scrumptious confections and savoury offerings. But how did the afternoon tea come about?

Afternoon tea evolved from the time of Queen Victoria and her ladies-in-waiting, who felt a bit hungry in the late afternoon, and began taking tea and small, light foods such as breads or biscuits. This became a daily gathering to share gossip and news and relax with friends. As the tea was served on low tables in the queen's parlour, it was called a 'low' tea.

There is also a 'high tea' that includes meats and a 'cream tea' with tea and scones. Finally, there's a 'royal tea' that includes champagne or sherry (or any type of alcohol these days). A typical tea service consists of a set of cups and saucers, small plates, and a teapot, sugar bowl and milk jug.

The 'proper' way to stir tea is backwards and forwards, not in a circle. Shockingly, Professor Dolores Umbridge does not follow this rule when she stirs the pink sugar into her cup with a circular motion.

This deluxe cookbook offers recipes for nibbles, sweets and brews that the seventh Duchess of Bedford would welcome warmly at her parlour gatherings. And you won't need Divination professor Sybill Trelawney to read your tea leaves to predict how much you and your guests will enjoy the magic of a Harry Potter–inspired afternoon tea.

CHAPTER ONE

SWEET FINGER TREATS AND SUGARY NIBBLES

'FUDGE HAS TO SEE BUCKBEAK BEFORE WE STEAL HIM – OTHERWISE HE'LL THINK HAGRID SET HIM FREE.'

– Hermione Granger to Harry Potter

Harry Potter and the Prisoner of Azkaban

HAGRID'S PUMPKIN TEATIME MADELEINES

V ✦ YIELD: 12 SERVINGS

Hagrid's pumpkin patch, created for *Harry Potter and the Prisoner of Azkaban*, provided a place for his Hippogriff, Buckbeak, to rest before the creature's execution – and for Buckbeak to be saved by Harry and Hermione when she uses the Time-Turner for his rescue. The moulds for the smaller pumpkins were used again to create pumpkin-shaped chocolate cakes for the dessert feast in *Harry Potter and the Goblet of Fire*.

These custard-based teatime cakes use a classic madeleine recipe with a twist inspired by Hagrid's pumpkin patch. After the pumpkin-cinnamon-flavoured madeleines bake, they're scattered lightly with icing sugar. And they're the perfect size for a high tea bite.

130g butter, melted and cooled

135g plain flour

2 medium eggs

150g granulated sugar

115g canned pumpkin purée

1 teaspoon ground cinnamon

½ teaspoon cardamom

½ teaspoon nutmeg

Pinch salt

1 tablespoon icing sugar

SPECIALIST TOOLS

Madeleine tin

Preheat the oven to 190°C/170°C fan/Gas Mark 5.

Using 15g of the melted butter, coat each individual cavity in the madeleine tin with butter, coating the crevices and indentations well. Scatter with 10g of flour to lightly flour each mould.

In a large mixing bowl, beat the eggs and granulated sugar on a low speed until combined well.

Add in the pumpkin, cinnamon, cardamom, nutmeg and salt. Add the remaining 125g of flour, followed by the remaining 115g of butter. Stir with a mixing spoon just until thoroughly combined.

Fill each individual cavity of the madeleine tin with 2 tablespoons of the mixture. Place in the oven and bake until lightly browned on the edges, 15–20 minutes.

Remove the madeleines from the oven and set them on a wire rack to cool while still in their moulds. When the madeleines are cool, scatter each one with icing sugar.

Store in an airtight container at room temperature for 3–4 days.

JACOB KOWALSKI'S MINI TEATIME PACZKI

V ✦ YIELD: 20–25 SERVINGS

Paczki (the singular form being paczek) are bite-sized, deep-fried, sugar-coated pillowy Polish doughnuts. When No-Maj Jacob Kowalski visits the Steen National Bank in New York to ask for a bank loan to open his own bakery in *Fantastic Beasts and Where to Find Them*, he proudly opens a suitcase with a selection of his home-made pastries to show the bank manager, including paczki based on his grandmother's recipe.

Actor Dan Fogler, who portrays Jacob Kowalski, has a reason for thinking it was kismet he played the part of a baker for the film. 'I knew the character really well, because my grandfather was a baker,' Fogler explains. 'He had the best pumpernickel in New York; that's what he was known for.'

Traditionally, paczki are jam-packed with a sweet prune filling, but there are endless varieties to choose from, such as lemon curd, apples, raspberries or custard. These are filled with a honey-sweetened rum raisin compote.

FOR THE RUM RAISIN FILLING

450g raisins

500ml dark spiced rum

175g honey

TO MAKE THE RUM RAISIN FILLING

In a medium bowl, combine the raisins and rum, and allow to sit in an airtight container in the refrigerator for at least 1 hour or overnight.

In a small pan on a high heat, bring the raisin mixture and honey to the boil. Boil, stirring constantly, until the mixture thickens to the consistency of a fruit jam, 4–5 minutes. Remove from heat and set aside, uncovered, until the filling cools, about 1 hour.

CONTINUED ON PAGE 16

'YOU GOTTA TRY THE PACZKI. OKAY. IT'S MY GRANDMOTHER'S RECIPE. THE ORANGE ZEST. JUST … (SIGHS)'

– Jacob Kowalski

Fantastic Beasts and Where to Find Them

CONTINUED FROM PAGE 15

FOR THE PACZKI

375g plain flour, plus 250g for dusting

50g granulated sugar

7g active dry yeast (1 packet)

½ teaspoon salt

175ml full-fat milk

50g vegetable fat

2 small eggs, at room temperature

¼ teaspoon white rum

2 litres vegetable oil, plus extra for greasing

SPECIALIST TOOLS

Sugar thermometer

TO MAKE THE PACZKI

In the bowl of a stand mixer with the dough hook attachment, combine 250g of flour, the sugar, yeast and salt.

In a medium saucepan over a medium heat, combine the milk, vegetable fat and 125ml water until the mixture reaches 51.6°C on a sugar thermometer. Remove the mixture from the heat as soon as it reaches 51.6°C. If the milk mixture is hotter than 51.6°C, it will affect the yeast when it is combined with the flour and yeast mixture.

Add the milk mixture to the bowl of the stand mixer with the flour mixture. Mix everything together well, beating at medium speed for 1 minute. Stop to scrape the flour from the sides of the bowl into the dough mixture. Add 125g flour and beat for another minute. Add the eggs and beat into the mixture for 1 minute. Add the rum and beat into the mixture for 1 minute. The dough will be wet and very sticky.

Spread 125g of flour on the work surface. Knead the dough for 5 minutes. This step is very important. Kneading the dough helps distribute the yeast throughout. To knead the dough, use the palms of your hands to push the dough down on the work surface again and again, folding it over each time. Use the front or back of your hands. Keep pushing and folding repeatedly. If there is flour around the edges of your workspace, try to incorporate as little as possible into the dough as you knead.

Pour the oil into a large deep saucepan or casserole and use about ¼ teaspoon of oil to grease a large mixing bowl. Form the dough into a ball and place the dough in the bowl.

Turn the dough over so that both sides are

covered with the oil. Cover the bowl with a tea towel, and set it aside in a warm, dry place away from windows or a frequently opened refrigerator; or near a warm cooker, where the dough can rise for 1 hour. The dough will not rise much; however, it will rise a little.

On the work surface where you kneaded the dough, spread the remaining 125g of flour around to create a space to roll out the dough and cut it into round shapes. After 1 hour of resting, place the dough on the floured work surface. Push your fist into the dough to remove the air caused by the yeast and rising.

Use a rolling pin to roll out the dough to a 1cm thickness. Use a 5–7.5cm round biscuit cutter to cut out pieces of the dough. Set the pieces of dough on the work surface, covered by a tea towel, to rise again, about 1 hour. The dough will not rise noticeably but will rise a little, which is enough.

While the dough is rising, heat the oil in the saucepan to 190°C/170°C fan/Gas Mark 5. Use the sugar thermometer to monitor the temperature. It is very important not to exceed 190°C/170°C fan/Gas Mark 5. If the oil is too hot, the dough can burn before the paczki are cooked all the way through.

Place 3 or 4 pieces of dough at a time in the oil, frying them until they are golden brown all round on the outside, 1–2 minutes on each side.

Use a slotted spoon to pull each of the paczki out and set them on a plate lined with kitchen paper.

When the paczki and the rum raisin filling have cooled enough to touch, fill the paczki with the rum raisin filling. Fill a piping bag with the rum raisin filling. Use a knife to poke a hole in the top of each paczek, and use the piping bag to squeeze about 1 tablespoon of the filling into each of the paczki.

Store at room temperature in an airtight container for 2–3 days.

> '... THAT'S WHY I WANT TO MAKE PASTRIES. YOU KNOW. IT MAKES PEOPLE HAPPY.'
>
> – Jacob Kowalski
>
> *Fantastic Beasts and Where to Find Them*

V ✦ YIELD: 8 SERVINGS

HOGWARTS HIGH TABLE ROASTED APPLE SCONE BITES WITH FRESH CREAM AND MINT

There were many feasts of main courses served in the Great Hall throughout the Harry Potter films, especially the Hogwarts welcome feast. So, set decorator Stephenie McMillan tried something new when welcoming the visiting students from Durmstrang and Beauxbatons for the Triwizard Tournament in *Harry Potter and the Goblet of Fire*: a dessert feast. Some of these puddings were completely edible, and others were not, depending on what could stay fresh under the hot film lights.

Scones were a must at Queen Victoria's afternoon teatimes and would have been a perfect addition to the Triwizard Tournament welcome feast (and they wouldn't melt under the lights!). This bite-sized take on the larger classic adds even more flavour to the feast, filled with roasted apples, cut into the shape of tart slices and topped with a sprig of fresh mint.

FOR THE APPLE MIXTURE

100g fresh apples, peeled and chopped into 1cm pieces

50g soft light brown sugar

Juice from ½ lemon

55g butter

FOR THE SCONE MIXTURE

375g plain flour, plus extra for dusting

1 tablespoon baking powder

½ teaspoon bicarbonate of soda

½ teaspoon salt

225g butter, cut into small pieces

1 egg

250g natural yogurt

½ teaspoon vanilla extract

2 teaspoons milk

1 teaspoon coarse sugar, for scattering on top of the scones

FOR THE FRESH CREAM TOPPING

500ml double cream

100g granulated sugar

¼ teaspoon fresh lemon juice

FOR THE GARNISH

6–8 sprigs fresh pineapple mint

✦ BEHIND THE MAGIC ✦

Among Stephenie McMillan's favourite sweets were the ice mice and the chocolate rabbits that leapt out of top hat cakes.

TO MAKE THE APPLE MIXTURE

Preheat the oven to 200°C/180°C fan/Gas Mark 6. In a large mixing bowl, toss the apples in the brown sugar and lemon juice. Allow to sit for at least 1 hour.

Place the apples in a frying pan in the oven with the butter until softened and browned around the edges, 15–20 minutes. Stir every 5 minutes.

Remove the apples from the oven and let sit on the work surface until cooled to room temperature.

TO MAKE THE SCONE MIXTURE

In a large mixing bowl, combine the flour, baking powder, bicarbonate of soda and salt. Add the butter, and use your hands to mix everything together until it turns to coarse crumbs. Add the egg, yogurt and vanilla, and continue to mix together until combined well.

When the roasted apples have cooled, add the apple mixture to the flour mixture. Save 175ml of the apple mixture to place a dab on top of each scone when they are served. Knead the dough 4 times to incorporate the apples.

Scatter 2 tablespoons of flour on the work surface. Place the dough on the work surface, and knead the dough 4–5 times.

Using your hands, press the dough into a 23–25cm circle. Cut the dough into 8 tart slices. Place the slices on an ungreased baking sheet. Brush the tops of each scone with the milk; scatter coarse sugar on top of each scone.

Bake until golden brown, about 15 minutes.

TO MAKE THE FRESH CREAM TOPPING

In the bowl of a stand mixer or a large mixing bowl with a hand mixer, beat the double cream, sugar and lemon juice together on low until well combined and starting to thicken so it won't splatter, about 3 minutes. Increase the speed to high and beat until thickened enough to form soft peaks, 12–15 minutes.

Serve the scones warm, with each scone topped with a dab of the apple mixture, a dollop of the cream and a sprig of the fresh mint.

Store the scones in an airtight container at room temperature for 3–4 days. Store the whipped cream in an airtight container in the refrigerator for 1–2 days.

'LET THE FEAST BEGIN!'

– Albus Dumbledore

Harry Potter and the Philosopher's Stone

DIVINATION DREAM BAR TEA TREATS

V ✦ YIELD: 24 SERVINGS

The first lesson Professor Trelawney teaches her third-year students is dream interpretation, which offers the possibility of predicting the future. Actress Emma Thompson describes her character's entrance into her classroom as 'one of the oldest, cheapest gags in the book,' for just as she announces that she has 'the Sight,' she walks into a table. She does this again, in *Harry Potter and the Prisoner of Azkaban*, when explaining the importance of dream interpretation, 'for the inner eye sees sights to which the outer world is blind'. As Trelawney says she sees into the future, it occurred to Thompson that she probably couldn't see anything at all in the present.

Dream bars – also known as 'magic bars' – are classic seven-layer bars. These are made with butterscotch chips, chopped walnuts and toasted coconut. A prediction for the future? You'll want to make these again and again.

- 130g butter, at room temperature, plus extra for greasing
- 135g plain flour
- 325g soft brown sugar
- 2 eggs
- ½ teaspoon baking powder
- ¼ teaspoon salt
- 1 teaspoon vanilla extract
- 85g chocolate chips
- 85g butterscotch chips
- 100g desiccated coconut
- 125g walnuts, chopped

Preheat the oven to 180°C/160°C fan/Gas Mark 4.

Grease a 23 x 33 cake tin with 15g of butter.

To make the base, in a large bowl, combine 125g of flour, 100g of brown sugar, and the remaining 115g of butter, and mix together with a hand-held pastry blender until combined well and the dough reaches a coarse consistency. Press the base dough across the bse of the greased cake tin, and bake until slightly brown, 20–25 minutes.

Remove the base layer from the oven, and set aside to cool on a wire rack. Leave the oven on for when the base layer is returned to bake with the top layer.

In a large bowl, beat the eggs slightly. Add the remaining 225g of brown sugar, the remaining 10g of flour, the baking powder, salt, vanilla, chocolate chips, butterscotch chips, coconut and walnuts. Stir until they are well combined.

Spread the topping mixture over the baked base evenly, ensuring the same amount of thickness throughout.

Bake the bars until they are browned on top and around the edges and they begin to pull away from the sides of the pan, about 15 minutes.

Let the bars cool on a wire rack. When they are cool, use a knife to cut them into 2.5cm squares.

Store in an airtight container at room temperature for 3–4 days.

✦ MUGGLE MAGIC ✦

Dream bars emerged in popularity in New York City and throughout the United States in the 1930s. They are a creamy, gooey, tasty confection that should be a must at teatime.

> 'IN THIS ROOM, YOU SHALL EXPLORE THE NOBLE ART OF DIVINATION.'
>
> – Sybill Trelawney
>
> *Harry Potter and the Prisoner of Azkaban*

GF, V ✦ YIELD: 8–10 SERVINGS

AUNT PETUNIA'S TEATIME WINDTORTE PUDDING

It is awful that the day Vernon Dursley may make the biggest deal of his career by entertaining the Masons at a dinner party, Dobby the house-elf appears, trying to prevent Harry from returning to Hogwarts. Noticing the colourful Windtorte pudding Petunia Dursley has baked for their guests, Dobby seizes the opportunity to cause trouble. Snapping his fingers, he floats the pudding from the kitchen to the living room and drops it on top of Mrs Mason.

The pudding that drifts in the direction of the Dursleys' guests was computer generated, but it was a real meringue-based pudding with whipped cream and sugared violets that fell on to actress Veronica Clifford's (Mrs Mason's) head.

This Windtorte pudding is inspired by that fateful moment in *Harry Potter and the Chamber of Secrets* and served how it appears in the film, as one pudding. We do, however, recommend enjoying the layers of meringue instead of dropping this pudding on anyone.

FOR THE MERINGUES

4 medium egg whites

100g granulated sugar

¼ teaspoon cream of tartar

FOR THE WHIPPED CREAM

500ml double cream

100g granulated sugar

½ teaspoon fresh lemon juice

TO MAKE THE MERINGUES

Preheat the oven to 180°C/160°C fan/Gas Mark 4. Line three 23 x30cm baking sheets with baking paper.

In the bowl of a stand mixer or with a hand mixer and a large mixing bowl, beat the egg whites, sugar and cream of tartar until thickened and peaks form.

On one of the baking sheets, spread the meringue in a circle about the size of a 23cm round cake tin. Repeat with the other two baking sheets. Bake the three meringue rounds for about 50 minutes, until brown on top and firm. Remove from the oven, leave on the baking sheets and place on the work surface to cool until they are room temperature.

TO MAKE THE WHIPPED CREAM

In the bowl of a stand mixer or with a hand mixer and a large mixing bowl, beat the double cream, sugar and lemon juice together on low until well combined and starting to thicken so that it won't splatter, about 3 minutes. Increase the speed to high and beat until thickened enough to form soft peaks, 12–15 minutes.

CONTINUED ON PAGE 25

CONTINUED FROM PAGE 23

FOR THE BUTTERCREAM ICING

750g icing sugar

225g butter, softened

2 teaspoons vanilla extract

60ml milk

FOR THE TOPPINGS

20 drops green food colouring

10 drops purple food colouring

15–20 edible or silk purple violets

30 maraschino cherries

✦ MUGGLE MAGIC ✦

Windtorte pudding is often called 'the fanciest cake in Vienna', which might be the reason Petunia baked this!

'THEN DOBBY MUST DO IT, SIR, FOR HARRY POTTER'S OWN GOOD.'

– Dobby the house-elf to Harry Potter

Harry Potter and the Chamber of Secrets

TO MAKE THE BUTTERCREAM ICING

In a large mixing bowl, use a hand mixer to combine the icing sugar, butter, vanilla and milk. Beat on high speed, until the icing is thick but is still soft enough to work with using a piping bag, about 10 minutes.

TO ASSEMBLE

Place one of the round meringues on a cake plate. Spread ⅓ of the whipped cream on top of this first layer of meringue. Place another meringue cake on top, and top with another ⅓ of the whipped cream. Place a third meringue cake on top, and top with the remaining ⅓ of the whipped cream.

Divide the icing in half, and place each half into separate medium mixing bowls. Add 20 drops of green food colouring to one half of the icing and 10 drops of purple food colouring to the other half. Mix in the food colourings in until thoroughly combined and there are no colour streaks.

Place each of the coloured icings into its own piping bag: put the bag into a cup and roll the edges over the rim of the cup to make it easier to fill the bag. Using a star nozzle in each bag, pipe dollops of icing all around the base layer of meringue. Pipe alternating dollops of green- and lavender-coloured icing all around the middle layer of meringue. Pipe dollops of lavender-coloured icing all around the top layer of meringue. Arrange edible or silk purple violets and maraschino cherries around the top and base layers of meringue.

Store in an airtight container in the refrigerator for 1–2 days, although it's best if eaten immediately after assembly.

V ✦ YIELD: 12 SERVINGS

HUNGARIAN HORNTAIL MINI TEATIME CAKES

For the first task of the Triwizard Tournament in *Harry Potter and the Goblet of Fire*, the four champions must acquire a golden egg from the clutches of a dragon – Harry's is a fire-breathing Hungarian Horntail, with spikes from its head to its tail.

The dragon Harry fought in the skies above Hogwarts was digital, but the film-makers asked for an animatronic version for Harry to encounter the night before the task. About 12 metres of Hungarian Horntail was created with a head featuring movable eyes, eyelids and nostrils. It also breathed fire: the Horntail's head was cast in fibreglass and outfitted with a fireproof snout. A flamethrower in the dragon's mouth shot an 11-metre stream of dragon's fire at the camera.

These miniature cakes are covered with an orange-coloured buttercream icing, then topped with home-made hard sweets that evoke the flames of a dragon's fire. But don't worry – these cupcakes are much sweeter than any fire-breathing dragon!

FOR THE CUPCAKES

255g butter, softened

400g granulated sugar

4 eggs, at room temperature

375g plain flour

1 tablespoon baking powder

250ml milk, at room temperature

2 teaspoons vanilla extract

TO MAKE THE CUPCAKES

Preheat the oven to 180°C/160°C fan/Gas Mark 4. Butter the cavities of a 12-hole muffin tin with 30g of butter, making sure the base and sides are completely covered.

In a large mixing bowl, using a handheld mixer at medium speed, beat the remaining 225g of butter and the sugar until the mixture becomes light and fluffy, about 4 minutes.

One at a time, add the eggs to the butter and sugar mixture. After each egg is added, beat until combined well.

Place the flour and baking powder in a separate medium bowl, and use a mixing spoon to stir them together.

CONTINUED ON PAGE 28

CONTINUED FROM PAGE 27

FOR THE BUTTERCREAM ICING

750g icing sugar

225g butter, softened

2 teaspoons vanilla extract

60ml milk

20 drops orange food colouring

FOR THE SUGAR FLAME TOPPERS

400g granulated sugar

160g golden syrup

5 drops red food colouring

5 drops yellow food colouring

5 drops orange food colouring

SPECIALIST TOOLS

Piping bag and medium round cake decorating nozzle

Sugar thermometer

Add ¼ of the flour mixture to the butter mixture, followed by 60ml of the milk. After each addition, beat the ingredients until they are mixed together well, about 1 minute. Repeat this three more times until all of the flour mixture and milk are mixed well. Add the vanilla, and beat to combine well, about 1 minute.

Fill each of the 12 cavities of the muffin tin ⅔ full with the mixture. Be careful not to over-fill the holes, or the mixture will expand over the sides while baking. Place the muffin tin in the oven and bake the puddings until the edges start to brown and pull away from the tin and a knife or skewer comes out clean when inserted in the centre, 30–35 minutes.

Remove the puddings from the oven and set aside to cool, about 1 hour.

TO MAKE THE BUTTERCREAM ICING

In a large mixing bowl, use a hand mixer to combine the icing sugar, butter, vanilla, milk and food colouring. Beat on a high speed until the icing is thick but is still soft enough to work with using a piping bag, about 10 minutes.

TO MAKE THE SUGAR FLAME TOPPERS

In a small saucepan over a high heat, combine the sugar with 175ml of water. Stir constantly until the sugar dissolves; add the golden syrup. Stir to combine thoroughly. Bring the mixture to the boil until it reaches the hard-crack stage (149–154°C), 7–8 minutes. Use a sugar thermometer to monitor the temperature of the mixture.

Separate the mixture into 3 small aluminium pans, and blend 5 drops of a food colouring into each pan: red, yellow and orange.

Line 2 baking sheets with baking paper. Using a separate large spoon for each colour, quickly drizzle each of the sugar mixtures on to the baking sheets. Spread the sugar mixture to make pieces in a variety of widths and lengths. Use a round-bladed knife to trace lines in the sugar flames. Add more drops of food colouring in spots to create more three-dimensional detail.

Let the sugar flames rest until they are hard enough to stand upright on their own in the icing of the puddings, 6–8 minutes.

When the puddings have cooled to room temperature, spread each one with the buttercream icing, and top each pudding with a sugar flame topper.

Store in an airtight container at room temperature for 2–3 days.

> 'WHAT'S LIFE WITHOUT A FEW DRAGONS?'
>
> – Ron Weasley
>
> *Harry Potter and the Goblet of Fire*

✦ BEHIND THE MAGIC ✦

The Hungarian Horntail's beak was made of steel that unintentionally but happily glowed red when the fire was released.

'I'M SURE WE'RE ALL GOING TO BE VERY GOOD FRIENDS.'

'THAT'S LIKELY.'

– Dolores Umbridge and a sarcastic Fred and George Weasley

Harry Potter and the Order of the Phoenix

PROFESSOR UMBRIDGE'S LOAD OF WAFFLES

V ✦ YIELD: 12 SERVINGS

Professor Dolores Umbridge starts her tenure at Hogwarts by interrupting Dumbledore and making her own speech at the welcome feast in Harry's fifth year. Her words are chilling and reflect the Ministry of Magic's attempt to interfere at Hogwarts. Harry called it 'a load of waffle.'

The Scottish-originated idiom 'a load of waffle' describes a speech that uses a lot of words but does not give any meaningful information. Although Umbridge is a bit obscure in this speech, she makes other things very clear: She doesn't like children, and she doesn't believe Harry Potter's assertion that Voldemort is back.

These mini waffles are dipped in maple syrup and scattered with coarse sugar so that guests can eat them with their fingers. The waffle mixture is made with soured cream, to reflect Professor Umbridge's sour personality.

- 5 medium eggs
- 100g granulated sugar
- 125g plain flour
- 1 teaspoon salt
- ¼ teaspoon ground cardamom
- ¼ teaspoon ground cinnamon
- ¼ teaspoon ground ginger
- 365g soured cream or or crème fraîche
- 60g butter, melted, plus extra for waffle iron
- 2 cups maple syrup
- 200g coarse sugar

SPECIALIST TOOLS

Mini heart-shaped waffle iron

In a large mixing bowl and with a hand mixer, beat the eggs and sugar until thoroughly combined, about 3 minutes.

In a separate large mixing bowl, mix the flour, salt, cardamom, cinnamon and ginger. Fold the egg mixture into the flour mixture. Add the soured cream or crème fraîche, combine thoroughly and add the melted butter.

Heat and butter the waffle iron. Pour in 320ml of the mixture for each waffle. Follow the instructions for the waffle iron to know when the waffle is done.

Pour the maple syrup on a large plate. Place the sugar on a separate large plate. While each waffle is still warm, but cool enough to touch, dip both sides of each waffle into the syrup, followed by the coarse sugar. Serve on a platter 'loaded' with waffles.

Store in an airtight container in the refrigerator for 2–3 days. To reheat, preheat the oven to 190°C/170°C fan/Gas Mark 5. Place the waffles on a baking sheet in a single layer, and put them in the oven until crispy again around the edges and hot throughout, 20–25 minutes.

✦ BEHIND THE MAGIC ✦

Actress Imelda Staunton feels Umbridge believes everything she does in her work is in the right. 'And what is more frightening than those people who don't question their jobs and just carry on and do it, regardless?'

V ✦ YIELD: 12 SERVINGS

PARIS PÂTISSERIE TWO-BITE LAVENDER TEATIME CANELÉS

In *Fantastic Beasts: The Crimes of Grindelwald*, Newt Scamander casts the tracking spell *Avenseguim* in Paris to locate the mysterious wizard Yusuf Kama. Newt and Jacob Kowalski wait for him at a café in the Place Cachée.

'Paris at this time was just such an extraordinary part of the world,' says actor Eddie Redmayne (Newt). 'It was where a melting pot of people were meeting, and new paths were being forged. This was really a time of change, a change in fashion, a change in architecture. It was an incredibly colourful and vibrant place.'

Canelés, like these, surged in popularity in late 1920s Paris. It's important that copper moulds are used as they're the best conductors of heat, to give these biscuits a crispy shell. Beeswax and butter are the traditional ways of greasing the moulds and give these treats a light, crunchy coating that seals in a moist, creamy, custardy centre with a hint of lavender and rum.

725ml milk
½ vanilla pod, split lengthways and scraped (or ¼ teaspoon vanilla extract)
210g butter
200g granulated sugar
85g plain flour
2 medium eggs
1 medium egg yolk
3 tablespoons rum
1 tablespoon chopped fresh or dried lavender buds
75g beeswax, finely chopped

In a small saucepan over a high heat, combine the milk and vanilla. Bring to the boil, then remove from heat. Add 40g of butter; stir to combine. Set aside to cool.

In a large mixing bowl, use a wire whisk to whisk together the sugar and flour.

CONTINUED ON PAGE 35

CONTINUED FROM PAGE 33

SPECIALIST TOOLS

Canelé moulds

Pastry brush

> 'I WAS SAYING – YOU SURE THE GUY'S HERE THAT WE'RE LOOKING FOR?'
>
> 'DEFINITELY. THE FEATHER SAYS SO.'
>
> – Jacob Kowalski and Newt Scamander
>
> *Fantastic Beasts: The Crimes of Grindelwald*

In a separate large mixing bowl, use a wire whisk to whisk together the 2 eggs, the egg yolk and rum. Next, whisk the egg mixture into the sugar and flour mixture; then whisk in the milk mixture. Add the lavender buds (saving a few for garnishing), and stir into the mixture. Pour the mixture into an airtight container and refrigerate overnight.

In a small saucepan over a low heat, melt the beeswax and add the remaining 170g of butter. Stir the wax and butter together while the mixture heats. Once it is well blended, remove from heat. Using a pastry brush, brush the insides of the canelé moulds with the mixture.

Remove the mixture from the refrigerator at least 1 hour before baking.

Preheat the oven to 220°C/200°C fan/Gas Mark 7.

Pour the mixture into the moulds. Fill each mould only half-full, to create mini canelés.

Bake until the canelés are dark brown, about 1 hour. Remove the moulds from the oven, and remove each canelé from its mould. Set them upright on a wire rack to cool. Store in an airtight container at room temperature for 2–3 days.

PROFESSOR McGONAGALL'S TRANSFIGURATIONAL STICKY TOFFEE PUDDING BITES

V ✦ YIELD: 12 SERVINGS

Professor McGonagall is head of Gryffindor house, the Transfiguration professor, and places the Sorting Hat on first-years' heads. She is also an Animagus, a witch or wizard who can change their form into that of a specific animal. McGonagall's feline form was played by a cat who already had spectacle-shaped markings around her eyes.

Crystallised ginger, apple and citrus transform this classic British dessert into a light, bright sticky toffee pudding. Sticky pudding is sticky inside and out – inside are Medjool dates blended with brown sugar and molasses to create a gooey filling spiced with nutmeg and cardamom. And the outside is drizzled with a thick, sweet sauce made with brown sugar and Scotch whisky.

Although bite-sized and tiny enough to fit on a three-tiered tea tray, these puddings should be served on individual plates because the toffee sauce can get a bit messy and transfigure other teatime bites into just-as-sticky nibbles.

FOR THE PUDDINGS

- 90g butter, at room temperature
- 150g Medjool dates, trimmed and pitted
- 1 teaspoon bicarbonate of soda
- 250ml boiling water
- 30g diced apple
- 20g crystallised ginger
- Juice of ½ medium orange
- 225g soft brown sugar
- ½ teaspoon vanilla extract
- 2 medium eggs, at room temperature
- 2 tablespoons molasses

TO MAKE THE PUDDINGS

Preheat the oven to 180°C/160°C fan/Gas Mark 4. Use the 15g of butter to grease the cavities of a 12-hole muffin tin. In a food processor, add the dates and bicarbonate of soda, then pour the boiling water over top. Set aside to soak for about 20 minutes.

In a large bowl, mix together the apples, ginger, orange juice, remaining 75g of butter, the brown sugar, vanilla, eggs and molasses until thoroughly combined.

In another large bowl, mix together the flour, baking powder, salt, nutmeg and cardamom. Combine the flour mixture with the apple mixture.

Pulse the dates, water and bicarbonate of

CONTINUED ON PAGE 38

CONTINUED FROM PAGE 37

- 200g plain flour
- 1½ teaspoons baking powder
- ¼ teaspoon salt
- ¼ teaspoon freshly grated nutmeg
- ¼ teaspoon cardamom
- 12 pointed ice-cream cones
- 1 tablespoon black cocoa powder

FOR THE SCOTCH WHISKY TOFFEE SAUCE

- 125ml double cream
- 115g butter
- 225g light brown sugar
- 1 tablespoon Scotch whisky
- 1 teaspoon vanilla extract
- 1 pinch pink Himalayan sea salt

FOR THE FRESHLY WHIPPED CREAM TOPPING

- 500ml double cream
- 100g granulated sugar
- ½ teaspoon fresh lemon juice

SPECIALIST TOOLS

Witch hat–shaped edible cupcake toppers or the pointed ends of ice-cream cones

soda until the dates become the consistency of a smooth purée; carefully fold the dates into the mixture.

Fill each of the cavities of the prepared muffin tin ¾ full with the mixture. Bake for about 20 minutes or until a toothpick inserted into the centre comes out clean.

TO MAKE THE SCOTCH WHISKY TOFFEE SAUCE

In a saucepan over a high heat, combine the double cream, butter, brown sugar, Scotch whisky, vanilla and salt. Stir to combine well and dissolve the sugar. Bring the mixture to the boil, stirring constantly, and boil for 1 minute.

Reduce the heat to medium-low and continue to cook until the sauce is smooth and slightly thick, 3–5 minutes.

TO MAKE THE FRESHLY WHIPPED CREAM TOPPING

In the bowl of a stand mixer or a large mixing bowl and a hand mixer, beat the double cream, sugar and lemon juice until the cream is thick, 12–15 minutes. Beat on a low speed for the first 2–3 minutes until the cream begins to thicken.

TO ASSEMBLE EACH DESSERT

Place a pudding upside down on a dessert plate. Use a dry pastry brush to dust the sugar cone hats with the black cocoa powder and top each pudding with a cone hat or an edible witch hat cupcake decoration. Drizzle the sauce over the ice-cream-cone top and the pudding; top each dessert with a dollop of the fresh whipped cream.

Store the sauce and the puddings, separately, in airtight containers in the refrigerator for 4–5 days.

'THAT WAS BLOODY BRILLIANT!'

– Ron Weasley in response to Professor McGonagall's transformation from a cat

Harry Potter and the Philosopher's Stone

V ✦ YIELD: 6 SERVINGS

MOLLY WEASLEY'S INDIVIDUAL TEATIME RHUBARB AND CUSTARD TRIFLES

Molly Weasley makes sure her family is well-fed – from eggs for breakfast to an elaborate turkey dinner for Christmas. Sharp eyes will notice a stack of cookbooks in The Burrow, including *One Minute Feasts – It's Magic!*, *Enchantment in Baking* and *Charm Your Own Cheese*, created by the graphics department.

These creamy trifles are similar to a rhubarb fool. However, this delicious trifle has layers of rhubarb sauce and custardy cream, a much-loved combination. Trifles are traditional at teatime, and their presentation adds to the variety of the tea, which is one of the most important aspects of entertaining during teatime.

Serve these in clear glass champagne flutes or wine glasses so that the pretty layers of roasted rhubarb, fresh cream and shortbread crumbles are visible to your guests. For even smaller portions, they can be served in clear shot glasses or timbales.

FOR THE ROASTED RHUBARB

275g trimmed rhubarb, chopped into 1cm pieces

50g soft brown sugar

1 tablespoon plain flour

NOTE ✦ When rhubarb is not in season, substitute 650g apricot jam or marmalade at room temperature.

TO MAKE THE ROASTED RHUBARB

Preheat the oven to 180°C/160°C fan/Gas Mark 4. Line a baking sheet with baking paper.

In a cast-iron frying pan, combine the rhubarb, brown sugar and flour, and stir until the rhubarb is thoroughly coated with the sugar-flour mixture. Place the frying pan in the oven and roast until the rhubarb mixture is soft and easily spreadable, 15–20 minutes. Remove from the oven and leave to cool until it is time to assemble the trifle.

CONTINUED ON PAGE 40

FOR THE SHORTBREAD BISCUITS

450g butter, softened

200g granulated sugar

4 teaspoons vanilla extract

500g plain flour

1 teaspoon salt

175g ground pecans (optional)

FOR THE FRESHLY WHIPPED CREAM LAYER

500ml double cream

100g granulated sugar

½ teaspoon fresh lemon juice

FOR THE VANILLA PUDDING LAYER

3 tablespoons cornflour

725ml full-fat milk, divided

¼ teaspoon pink Himalayan sea salt

200g sugar

3 egg yolks

15g butter, softened

1 vanilla pod, or ¼ teaspoon vanilla extract

FOR THE GARNISH

1 tablespoon chiffonade fresh mint leaves

1 tablespoon chopped fresh marjoram leaves

TO MAKE THE SHORTBREAD BISCUITS

In a large mixing bowl with a handheld mixer on a medium-high speed, cream together the butter, sugar, 2 tablespoons of water and the vanilla, gradually adding in the flour and salt. Cream until fluffy and light. Add the pecans, if using, and combine well.

Use a small ice-cream scoop to measure the mixture, and roll it in your hands to create 2.5cm-diameter balls. Place the biscuit balls 5cm apart on the prepared baking sheet. Use the palm of your hand to press down each ball to a 1cm thickness.

Bake until the edges of the biscuits are lightly browned, 20–25 minutes. Remove from the oven, and set aside to cool.

TO MAKE THE WHIPPED CREAM LAYER

In a stand mixer or a large mixing bowl with a hand mixer, beat together the double cream, sugar and lemon juice on a low speed until well combined and starting to thicken so it won't splatter, about 3 minutes. Increase the speed to high and beat until thick enough to form soft peaks, 12–15 minutes.

TO MAKE THE VANILLA PUDDING LAYER

In a large mixing bowl, whisk the cornflour with 60ml of the milk.

In a medium saucepan over a medium heat, whisk together the remaining 665ml of the milk, the salt and sugar. Cook, stirring occasionally, until there is steam.

In a medium bowl, whisk the egg yolks. Pour 125ml of the steamed milk into the egg yolks and stir constantly. Slowly place the egg mixture and cornflour mixture in the saucepan and simmer, whisking constantly, until the mixture thickens.

Using a knife, split the vanilla pod and scrape the vanilla seeds from the pod. Discard the pod. Set aside the seeds from the pod on a medium plate on the work surface.

Remove the pudding from the heat; stir in the butter and the seeds that was scraped from the inside of the vanilla pod.

TO ASSEMBLE THE TRIFLES

Using your hands, crush together two shortbread biscuits at a time until all of the biscuits are roughly crushed. Place 50g of the crushed biscuits into each of 6 clear wine glasses. Divide the pudding equally among the 6 glasses, placing it on top of the crushed biscuits, followed by the roasted rhubarb and the fresh whipping cream. Top each trifle with a scattering of fine biscuit crumbs and fresh mint and marjoram leaves.

Store the pudding, rhubarb mixture and whipped cream in separate airtight containers in the refrigerator for 1–2 days. Store the biscuits in an airtight container at room temperature for 4–5 days.

'YOU HUNGRY, HARRY?'

– Molly Weasley

Harry Potter and the Order of the Phoenix

✦ MUGGLE MAGIC ✦

'Fool' plays on the meaning of something described as a trifle as being inconsequential.

V ✦ YIELD: 6 BITE-SIZED OR 8 MINI PROFITEROLE SERVINGS

PROFESSOR SLUGHORN'S ONE-BITE HIGH TEA PROFITEROLES

In *Harry Potter and the Half-Blood Prince,* Potions professor Horace Slughorn hosts a dinner party for members of his newly revived 'Slug Club'. Dessert for the selected students is a heaped serving of mouth-watering profiteroles.

It's at this dinner that Cormac McLaggen tries to catch the attention of Hermione Granger by dipping his fingers into his bowl and cleaning them off as she watches in distress. The action was not in the script but improvised by actor Freddie Stroma as Cormac, on the suggestion of director David Yates.

Profiteroles are often served in the form of a tower, but this teatime version made with a basic pâte à choux recipe offers miniature choux buns filled with freshly whipped cream with a hint of lemon, topped with a minty chocolate sauce and garnished with a sprig of fresh chocolate mint. You won't need to lick your fingers clean like Cormac to woo your guests with these profiteroles.

FOR THE PÂTE À CHOUX

60g butter, at room temperature

60g plain flour

2 eggs, at room temperature

FOR THE CREAM FILLING

500ml double cream

100g granulated sugar

½ teaspoon fresh lemon juice

FOR THE MINTY CHOCOLATE SAUCE

115g mint milk chocolates

60g butter

1 tablespoon chiffonade fresh chocolate mint leaves

TO MAKE THE PÂTE À CHOUX

Preheat the oven to 200°C/180°C fan/Gas Mark 6. Line a baking sheet with baking paper.

In a large saucepan over a high heat, bring 60ml of water and the butter to the boil. When the water and butter start to boil, quickly add the flour and stir until the mixture forms a ball. Remove the mixture from the heat. Using a handheld mixer, beat the eggs in, one at a time, until the mixture is smooth.

Use a 2.5cm ice-cream scoop to form the mixture into balls, and place the balls 6cm apart from one another on the prepared baking sheet.

Bake until golden brown around the edges, 35–40 minutes. Remove them from the oven and set aside until they have cooled, about 30 minutes. Use a serrated knife to cut each of the pastries in half horizontally.

TO MAKE THE CREAM FILLING

In the bowl of a stand mixer or a large mixing bowl with a hand mixer, beat the whipping cream, sugar and lemon juice together on low until well combined and starting to thicken so it won't splatter, about 3 minutes. Increase the speed to high and beat the cream until thickened enough to form soft peaks, 12–15 minutes.

TO MAKE THE MINTY CHOCOLATE SAUCE

Melt the chocolate and butter in a heatproof bowl set over a saucepan of simmering water or melt in the microwave. If using the microwave, microwave in a microwave-safe bowl for 1 minute, stirring after 30 seconds.

Place the cream filling between the top and base pieces of each of the pastries. Drizzle 1 tablespoon of mint chocolate sauce over each profiterole, and garnish with the mint leaves.

Store the pastry and chocolate sauce in separate airtight containers at room temperature for 1–2 days. Store the cream filling in an airtight container in the refrigerator for 1–2 days.

'... JUST IN TIME FOR DESSERT. THAT IS, IF BELBY'S LEFT YOU ANY.'

– Horace Slughorn

Harry Potter and the Half-Blood Prince

✦ BEHIND THE MAGIC ✦

For the most part, the food seen on screen was faked, or a combination of both fake and real food, but as the students were actively eating the dessert, real profiteroles were served.

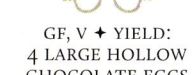

GF, V ✦ YIELD:
4 LARGE HOLLOW
CHOCOLATE EGGS

KOWALSKI BAKERY'S OCCAMY EGG TEATIME SURPRISE

Jacob Kowalski is turned down for a business loan in *Fantastic Beasts and Where to Find Them*, but his friendship with Newt Scamander compels the Magizoologist to gift him a case of Occamy eggshells as collateral to start his bakery. Occamy eggshells are made of the purest silver and worth a fortune.

This teatime treat, inspired by the Occamy eggs seen in the film, is a treat within a treat! Each white chocolate Occamy egg holds another sweet surprise inside. For example, you can put in one of Professor McGonagall's Transfigurational Sticky Toffee Pudding Bites or a Two-Bite Lavender Teatime Canelé inside. To resemble the Occamy eggs in the film, they're covered with edible silver cake-decorating dust. And so guests can crack open the egg, each is served with a small wooden mallet or a tool of your choice to find the confection nestled inside.

60g white chocolate chips

30g butter

1 tablespoon edible silver lustre dust

FOR THE FILLING

Any combination of the below:

Hagrid's Pumpkin Teatime Madeleines (page 13)

One-Bite Circus Animal Tea Biscuits (page 53)

Dumbledore's Elderberry Tea Pastilles (page 143)

Disenchantment Tea Jellies (page 133)

In a large microwave-safe bowl in the microwave or in a heat-proof bowl set over a saucepan of simmering water, melt the white chocolate chips and butter just until the chips are melted. Use a spoon to stir until the butter and white chocolate are blended together thoroughly. If melting the chocolate in the microwave, heat the chocolate on medium for 1 minute, stir, and heat for another 1 minute.

Using a pastry brush, coat the inside of each half of the egg moulds with lustre dust. Pour the melted chocolate into the mould and rotate it for smooth coverage. Pull the chocolate up along the sides to the top of the egg mould all around. Repeat this multiple times all around, until the inside of each mould is covered about 5mm thick with chocolate. Use a clean round-bladed knife to go around the edge of the mould, evening out the chocolate around the edges.

Place the mould in the refrigerator until the chocolate sets enough to stand on its own once the mould is removed, 10–15 minutes.

CONTINUED ON PAGE 47

CONTINUED FROM PAGE 45

SPECIALIST TOOLS

Large silicone egg mould
4 wooden mallets for cracking chocolate

'DEAR MR KOWALSKI. YOU ARE WASTED IN A CANNING FACTORY. PLEASE TAKE THESE OCCAMY EGGSHELLS AS COLLATERAL FOR YOUR BAKERY. A WELL-WISHER.'

– Note from Newt Scamander to Jacob Kowalski

Fantastic Beasts and Where to Find Them

✦ BEHIND THE MAGIC ✦

Occamys are *choranaptyxic*: creatures that shrink or grow according to the available space, a word created by the screenwriter, J K Rowling.

Remove the mould from the refrigerator, and pull the silicone mould away from the chocolate. Using a pastry brush, go around the edge of the top and base halves of the eggs with hot water so that the chocolate softens just enough so that both the two halves of the eggs will stick when they are brought together. Dust the outside of each half once more with lustre dust, if desired.

Place a tiny sweet treat in the middle of one of the egg halves (see options from Ingredients List page 45). Bring the egg halves together so that the edges line up, and lightly press until the halves are secured together, about 3 minutes. Place the eggs back in the refrigerator to harden together well, about 3 minutes.

Remove from the refrigerator, and allow the eggs sit until room temperature, about 5 minutes.

Place the edible silver lustre dust on a plate or in a shallow bowl. Roll the eggs in the dusting powder so that the powder completely covers the eggs. If enough powder does not stick, scatter the dust on top of the eggs when they are on a plate, ready to be served. Serve each egg with a mallet to open it.

Store the chocolate eggs in an airtight container at room temperature for 2–3 weeks.

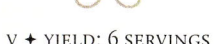

V ✦ YIELD: 6 SERVINGS

HONEYDUKES LEMON DROP MERINGUE TEATIME BITES

Within the film set for Honeydukes, seen in *Harry Potter and the Prisoner of Azkaban*, are jars and jars of Chocoballs and Exploding Bonbons, plus Liquorice Wands, toffees, and Jelly Slugs (they're 'wriggling good'). Tall glass dispensers of Bertie Bott's Every Flavour Beans line the mint-green walls, and there are rows of Chocolate Skeletons.

A particular favourite in the Honeydukes line of products is Sherbet Lemons. *Sherbet Lemon* is used by Albus Dumbledore as the password for access to his office, which Professor McGonagall intones in *Harry Potter and the Chamber of Secrets*.

Inspired by Honeydukes' Sherbet Lemons, these teatime bites are mini deconstructed lemon meringue tarts, without the crust. In the centre of the meringue is a bright, lemony home-made tart filling that tastes as refreshingly sharp and lemony as the lemony sweets at Honeydukes.

FOR THE MERINGUES

- 4 medium egg whites
- 50g granulated sugar
- ¼ teaspoon cream of tartar

'SHERBET LEMON'.

– The password to the Hogwarts headmaster's office spoken by Minerva McGonagall

Harry Potter and the Chamber of Secrets

TO MAKE THE MERINGUES

Preheat the oven to 180°C/160°C fan/Gas Mark 4. Line a baking sheet with baking paper.

In the bowl of a stand mixer or a large mixing bowl with a hand mixer on high speed, beat the egg whites, sugar, and cream of tartar until thick and peaks form, 12–15 minutes.

Use a large ice-cream scoop to scoop 2.5cm balls of the meringue, and place each ball of meringue on the prepared baking sheet about 4cm apart. Use a spoon to flatten each meringue to a 1cm thickness, and create a depression in the centre of each of the meringues where the lemon tart filling will be placed. Bake until slightly firm, enough to hold up the lemon pudding, about 50 minutes.

CONTINUED ON PAGE 50

CONTINUED FROM PAGE 49

FOR THE LEMON TART FILLING

- 200g granulated sugar
- 3 tablespoons cornflour
- 3 tablespoons plain flour
- ¼ teaspoon pink Himalayan sea salt
- 3 medium egg yolks, beaten, at room temperature
- Juice and zest of 3 lemons
- 15g butter

FOR THE FRESH WHIPPED CREAM

- 500ml double cream
- 100g granulated sugar
- ½ teaspoon fresh lemon juice

TO MAKE THE LEMON TART FILLING

In a saucepan over a high heat, combine the sugar, cornflour, flour, 300ml of water and the salt. Stir constantly until the mixture bubbles lightly and thickens. Add the egg yolks and bring the mixture to the boil. Stir constantly for 2 minutes. Reduce the heat to low, and add the lemon juice, zest and butter. Stir until blended well and there are no lumps.

TO MAKE THE FRESH WHIPPED CREAM

In the bowl of a stand mixer or a large mixing bowl with a hand mixer, beat the double cream, sugar and lemon juice until the cream is thickened, 12–15 minutes. Beat on a low speed for the first 2–3 minutes until the cream begins to thicken, then increase to high speed for the remaining 10–13 minutes.

To assemble, arrange the baked meringues on a serving platter. Use a spoon to put 2 tablespoons of lemon filling in a circle in the centre on top of each meringue. Spread the tart filling around in a circular motion, making sure that it forms a complete circle to resemble an egg yolk. Place a dollop of fresh whipped cream on the left side of each meringue, allowing the lemon pudding to be visible.

Store in an airtight container in the refrigerator for 1–2 days.

> ✦ **BEHIND THE MAGIC** ✦
>
> For filming inside the Honeydukes set, the actors were told that all the sweets had been coated with a lacquer finish, but it turned out that was just a story to keep them from eating them!

V ✦ YIELD: 80 BITE-SIZED BISCUITS

ONE-BITE CIRCUS ANIMAL TEA BISCUITS

Circus animal-based biscuits have been around since the dawn of the twentieth century. These whimsical tea biscuits, inspired by the magic of the Circus Arcanus where Tina Goldstein locates Credence Barebone in *Fantastic Beasts: The Crimes of Grindelwald*, are cut out in the shape of traditional Muggle circus animals and decorated in classic circus animal biscuit colours, featuring white and hot pink icing, with scatterings of sprinkles to add pops of colour, whimsy and nostalgia to the assortment.

In addition to the exotic beasts that are showcased at Circus Arcanus, there are also some unique street vendors. The candy floss stand has chin rests where the floss maker can magic a beard for patrons (a play on the French term for candy floss, *barbe à papa*, which translates to 'father's beard'). There are also candy floss–shaped balloons, with the idea being they don't have the normal gravitational issues, so the candy floss floats.

FOR THE BISCUITS

500g plain flour, plus extra for dusting

1 teaspoon bicarbonate of soda

1 teaspoon baking powder

200g vegetable fat

300g granulated sugar

1½ teaspoons salt

240g soured cream or crème frâiche

2 eggs, at room temperature

1 teaspoon vanilla extract

TO MAKE THE BISCUITS

Preheat the oven to 180°C/160°C fan/Gas Mark 4. Line a baking sheet with baking paper.

In a large bowl, combine the flour, bicarbonate of soda, baking powder, vegetable fat, sugar, salt, soured cream or crème frâiche, eggs and vanilla until well combined. Chill the mixture in the refrigerator for about 30 minutes.

Using a rolling pin, roll out the mixture on a floured work surface.

Use miniature circus animal-shaped biscuit cutters to cut out the biscuits.

Place the biscuits on the prepared baking sheet, about 4cm apart. Bake until lightly browned around the edges, about 10 minutes.

CONTINUED ON PAGE 55

NOTE ✦ Use biscuit cutters shaped like beasts or colour the biscuits with icing in unusual shades of purple or green, or mixes of both, to reflect the circus environment.

CONTINUED FROM PAGE 53

FOR THE ICING

125g icing sugar

2 tablespoons milk

4 drops red food colouring

100g multicoloured sprinkles

SPECIALIST TOOLS

Miniature circus animal biscuit cutters

TO MAKE THE ICING

In a large bowl, mix the icing sugar and milk together thoroughly until the icing becomes a smooth consistency.

Divide the icing in half, placing one half in a separate bowl, and add 4 drops of red food colouring to half of the icing.

One by one, dip half of the biscuits into the pink icing and the other half into the white icing. Quickly, before the icing begins to dry, scatter each biscuit with multicoloured sprinkles.

Store at room temperature in an airtight container for 2–3 weeks.

'CIRQUE ARCANUS: LE PLUS GRAND DES CIRQUES L'ÉVÉNEMENT DU SIÈCLE'

(CIRCUS ARCANUS: THE GREATEST CIRCUS EVENT OF THE CENTURY)

– Advertising Poster for Circus Arcanus

Fantastic Beasts: The Crimes of Grindelwald

'YOU PREFER STRUDEL. HUH? STRUDEL IT IS.'

– Legilimens Queenie Goldstein reading Jacob Kowalski's mind

Fantastic Beasts and Where to Find Them

GF*, V ✦ YIELD: 8 SERVINGS

QUEENIE'S MINI BRANDIED APPLE STRUDELS WITH APPLE MINT SAUCE

Queenie Goldstein uses magic to make a delicious apple strudel for Newt Scamander and Jake Kowalski when they visit the Goldstein sisters' flat in *Fantastic Beasts and Where to Find Them*. With a delicate wave of her wand, apples are sliced, then combined with raisins and spices before being wrapped in several layers of rolled dough. Dough roses and leaves land like butterflies on the pastry, all scattered with a generous helping of icing sugar.

Strudel means 'whirlwind' in this national dish of Austria, recognising the swirl of pastry and filling.

These teatime strudels are diminutive puff pastries filled with cinnamon-spiced apples cooked down with brandy and drizzled with a brandy-butter sauce. Each has a miniature plait, just like the plaited strudel Queenie makes.

FOR THE STRUDELS

- 4 large Jazz or Pink Lady apples, peeled and cut into 2.5cm pieces
- 75g raisins
- 250ml brandy
- 2 tablespoons soft brown sugar
- 1 tablespoon granulated sugar
- ¼ teaspoon ground cinnamon
- 60g walnuts, chopped
- 450g puff pastry, thawed if frozen
- 2 teaspoons butter
- 1 egg white

TO MAKE THE STRUDELS

Line a 23 x 30cm baking sheet with baking paper. Preheat the oven to 190°C/170°C fan/Gas Mark 5.

In a large bowl, marinate the apples and raisins in the brandy for 1–2 hours.

Strain the apples and raisins from the brandy over a large mixing bowl, reserving the brandy to make the sauce.

In a medium saucepan over a medium heat, combine the apples and raisins with the brown sugar, granulated sugar and cinnamon. Cook until thick, 8–10 minutes. Add the walnuts and stir to incorporate. Set aside to cool.

Cut the pastry into eight 10 x 5cm rectangles and 24 thin strips that are 10cm long. Create 8 plaits, one for each strudel: using three strips side by side, cross the left strip over the centre strip; then cross the right strip over the centre strip, alternating, until the full length of each strip is plaited.

CONTINUED ON PAGE 59

CONTINUED FROM PAGE 57

FOR THE CINNAMON-SUGAR TOPPING

4 tablespoons ground cinnamon

4 tablespoons sugar

FOR THE BRANDY-BUTTER SAUCE

1 tablespoon brown sugar

1 teaspoon butter

FOR THE GARNISH

40g fresh apple mint, chopped

NOTE ✦ For a gluten-free option, serve this apple filling and this sauce over a scoop of ice cream in a pretty glass dish, and garnish with a sprig of fresh apple mint.

✦ BEHIND THE MAGIC ✦

Texturing and shading were added digitally to Queenie's strudel that would mimic the appearance of the pastry cooking, and like most bakes while they cook, the animators had it shrink down a little.

When the apple mixture is cool, place 3 tablespoons of mixture on one side of each rectangular piece of pastry. Leave a 1cm border around the sides. Place ¼ teaspoon butter on top of the apple mixture on each piece of pastry. Fold the other side of each piece of pastry over the apple mixture. Use the tines of a fork to press down the pastry together on the three sides where the top and bottom come together.

Place one pastry plait on one of the long sides of each strudel rectangle; press down the top of the plait in the top corner of the strudel to secure the plait. The plait will extend over the base edge of the pastry by 1cm.

Lightly beat the egg white, and use a pastry brush to cover each strudel with the egg white.

Pierce the top of each strudel with a knife to create ventilation.

TO MAKE THE CINNAMON-SUGAR TOPPING

In a small bowl, combine the cinnamon and sugar.

Scatter the cinnamon-sugar mixture lightly on top of the strudels.

Place the strudels on the prepared baking sheet.

Bake until golden brown and flaky, 35–40 minutes. Remove from the oven and cool.

TO MAKE THE BRANDY-BUTTER SAUCE

In a small saucepan over a medium-high heat, combine the remainder of the brandy used for marinating the apples and raisins with the brown sugar and butter. Bring to the boil, stirring constantly, then reduce the heat to medium-low and simmer until thick, about 20 minutes. Remove the sauce from the heat.

Use a spoon to lightly drizzle the brandy-butter sauce over each strudel; garnish with fresh apple mint.

Store the sauce in the refrigerator in an airtight container for 5–6 days, and the strudels in the refrigerator in an airtight container for 3–4 days.

V ✦ YIELD: 12 SERVINGS

PROFESSOR SPROUT'S BITE-SIZED GREENHOUSE MYSTERY CAKES

It's possible that among the plant life Professor Sprout grows for her Herbology classes in *Harry Potter and the Chamber of Secrets* are lunch- and dinnertime staples such as tomatoes (which are a fruit!). Fortunately, tomatoes are a lot easier to work with than screaming Mandrakes or snapping Venomous Tentacula. The design of Greenhouse Three, where the second-years are taught, was inspired by a greenhouse at Kew Royal Botanic Gardens, built during the Victorian era, only a decade or so after regular afternoon teas began.

These mini puddings are a twist on the 1930s tomato soup cake, with its warming nutmeg, cinnamon and clove spiciness. The dessert was sometimes known as the mystery cake, because it would take a very discerning palate to recognise that the cake is made with a can of tomato soup! Each bite-sized pudding is capped with vanilla icing and then topped with a dollop of a sweet tomato jam.

FOR THE TOMATO SOUP PUDDINGS

15g butter, for greasing

3 tablespoons vegetable fat

200g granulated sugar

2 eggs

300g canned tomato soup

250g plain flour

1⅛ teaspoons bicarbonate of soda

1 teaspoon nutmeg

1 teaspoon cloves

1 teaspoon ground cinnamon

125g walnuts, chopped

150g raisins or chopped dates

FOR THE ICING

750g icing sugar

335g butter, softened

1 tablespoon vanilla extract

75ml full-fat milk

FOR THE TOMATO JAM

24 multicoloured cherry tomatoes

400g granulated sugar

2 tablespoons honey

1 tablespoon vanilla extract

'WELCOME TO GREENHOUSE THREE. SECOND-YEARS. NOW GATHER 'ROUND, EVERYONE.'

– Pomona Sprout

Harry Potter and the Chamber of Secrets

✦ MUGGLE MAGIC ✦

As a fun game, have your guests try to guess what the mystery ingredient is before it is revealed.

TO MAKE THE TOMATO SOUP PUDDINGS

Preheat the oven to 180°C/160°C fan/Gas Mark 4. Grease a 12-hole muffin tin with butter.

In a large mixing bowl, using a handheld mixer on a high speed, beat together the vegetable fat and sugar. Add the eggs and beat until well combined. Add the soup and beat until well combined. In a separate large mixing bowl, use a large mixing spoon to mix the flour, bicarbonate of soda, nutmeg, cloves and cinnamon. Add the walnuts and raisins. With the same spoon, add the flour mixture to the egg mixture, and stir to combine thoroughly. Place in the prepared muffin tin.

Bake until a skewer inserted in the middle of one of the cakes comes out clean, 35–40 minutes.

TO MAKE THE ICING

In a stand mixer or a large mixing bowl with a hand mixer on a high speed, combine the icing sugar, butter, vanilla and milk until combined thoroughly and thick yet spreadable, about 10 minutes.

TO MAKE THE TOMATO JAM

In a small saucepot over a high heat, combine the tomatoes, 500ml water, sugar, honey and vanilla, and bring to the boil. Reduce the heat to a medium-high, and stir occasionally until thick, 20–30 minutes.

When the cakes have cooled, top each one with icing. Serve with a dollop of tomato jam on top of each cake.

Store the cakes at room temperature in an airtight container for 3–4 days. Store the tomato jam in the refrigerator in an airtight container for 4–5 days.

PLACE CACHÉE ORANGE-SCENTED TEATIME PASTRY PUFFS

V ✦ YIELD: 24 SERVINGS

The Place Cachée (the hidden place) is the Parisian equivalent of Diagon Alley, except this version is actually two locations in one: a shopping area for Muggles and, at the same time, the same for magical folk, entered through a bronze statue of a robed woman in a way similar to Platform 9¾. In Diagon Alley, there is a cauldron shop, and so there is a French version featuring copper jelly moulds. There's also an apothecary, a wand shop and, of course, a pâtisserie (pastry shop): *Confiserie Enchantée*.

These diminutive orange-and-almond-flavoured pâte à choux pastries would be revered at any Parisian café. After being topped with an icing and flaked almonds, teatime guests can eat these with their fingers in one or two bites.

FOR THE BASE LAYER
125g plain flour
115g butter

FOR THE TOP LAYER
115g butter
1 teaspoon orange extract
125g plain flour
3 eggs

FOR THE ICING
750g icing sugar
335g butter, softened
75ml full-fat milk

FOR THE TOPPING
50g flaked almonds
½ teaspoon freshly grated orange zest

TO MAKE THE BASE LAYER

Preheat the oven to 190°C/170°C fan/Gas Mark 5. Line two 23 x 30cm baking sheets with baking paper. Use a fork or a handheld pastry blender to mix together the flour and butter. Add 2 tablespoons of water, spreading it evenly across the butter and flour mixture. Mix until a dough forms. Divide the dough in half, then form two long oval shapes, thinning the dough out to about 5mm thick all around the oval. Place each dough oval on its own baking sheet.

TO MAKE THE TOP LAYER

In a saucepan over a high heat, bring 250ml of water and the butter to the boil. Add the orange extract, remove the saucepan from the heat and add the flour. Stir until it starts to pull away from the edge of the saucepan. Add the eggs, one at a time, stirring each egg as it is added, until all 3 eggs are incorporated well.

Divide this mixture in half, and spread it evenly across the top of each of the base layers on the baking sheets.

Bake until golden brown around the edges, about 1 hour. Remove from the oven and set aside to cool.

TO MAKE THE ICING

In a stand mixer or a large mixing bowl with a hand mixer, combine the icing sugar, butter and milk until combined thoroughly and the icing is thick yet spreadable, about 10 minutes. Beat on a low speed for 1 minute to incorporate the ingredients, then increase to a high speed.

When the pastries have cooled to room temperature, spread the icing evenly across the top. Scatter the sliced almonds evenly across the top of each pastry before the icing dries. Scatter the orange zest on top of each pastry. Cut each pastry into 2.5–5cm square bite-sized pieces.

Store at room temperature in an airtight container for 2–3 days.

> *CONFISERIE ENCHANTÉE ~ DÉLICES SUCRÉS RAFFINÉS ~ SUBLIME BONBONS DELICATS*
>
> (ENCHANTED CONFECTIONARY ~ REFINED SWEET DELIGHTS ~ SUBLIME DELICIOUS SWEETS)
>
> – Signage for the *Confiserie Enchantée* on Place Cachée in Paris
>
> *Fantastic Beasts: The Crimes of Grindelwald*

✦ BEHIND THE MAGIC ✦

Although the shops on Place Cachée are never entered in *Fantastic Beasts: The Crimes of Grindelwald*, they are filled with merchandise.

'WELL, YOU ALL KNOW, OF COURSE, THAT HOGWARTS WAS FOUNDED OVER A THOUSAND YEARS AGO BY THE FOUR GREATEST WITCHES AND WIZARDS OF THE AGE: GODRIC GRYFFINDOR, HELGA HUFFLEPUFF, ROWENA RAVENCLAW AND SALAZAR SLYTHERIN.'

– Minerva McGonagall

Harry Potter and the Chamber of Secrets

V ✦ YIELD: 8–12 SERVINGS

HOGWARTS HOUSES FOUR-LAYER RAINBOW PETITS FOURS

Each layer of these multicoloured petits fours, inspired by one of the four houses of Hogwarts, explodes with a different flavour of tea and showcases the colours of the houses the students are sorted into at Hogwarts School of Witchcraft and Wizardry.

The red house colour of Gryffindor is distinguished by raspberry or strawberry tea. Slytherin is shaded green and tastes of Moroccan mint tea. Ravenclaw blue comes from the butterfly pea flower tea leaves and blue spirulina powder, and the yellow of Hufflepuff is made with lemon-lime tea. Each petit four is topped with a very light glaze, then scattered with edible gold dust and tiny stars.

FOR THE CAKES

- 255g butter, softened
- 400g sugar
- 4 eggs, at room temperature
- 375g plain flour
- 1 tablespoon baking powder
- 250ml milk, at room temperature
- 2 teaspoons vanilla extract
- 1 teabag raspberry or strawberry tea
- 1 teabag Moroccan mint tea
- 1 teabag lemon-lime tea
- 1 teabag butterfly pea flower tea

TO MAKE THE CAKES

Preheat the oven to 180°C/160°C fan/Gas Mark 4.

Butter four 20cm square cake tins with 30g of the softened butter.

In a large bowl with a handheld mixer at a medium speed, beat the remaining 225g of butter and the sugar together until the mixture becomes light and fluffy, about 4 minutes.

One at a time, add the eggs to the mixture. After each egg is added, beat until combined well.

Place the flour and baking powder in a separate medium bowl, and use a spoon to stir them together.

Add ⅓ of the flour mixture to the butter mixture, followed by ⅓ of the milk; repeat this two more times until both are completely added to the butter mixture. After each addition, beat until mixed together well, about 1 minute. Add the vanilla and beat to combine well, about 1 minute.

CONTINUED ON PAGE 66

CONTINUED FROM PAGE 65

- 2 teaspoons blue spirulina powder
- 25 drops yellow liquid food colouring
- 20 drops red liquid food colouring
- 12 drops green liquid food colouring

FOR THE CAKE FILLING LAYER

- 300g elderberry jam

FOR THE ICING

- 250g icing sugar
- 4 tablespoons milk

FOR THE GARNISH

- Edible gold dust and stars

Divide the cake mixture into 4 equal parts and place each part into a separate 20cm square cake tin. Using scissors, open up each of the teabags by cutting across the top. Mix each of the four parts of mixture with one of the teas and food colouring, and stir to combine well: mix one with the raspberry or strawberry tea and the red food colouring; one with the Moroccan mint tea and the green food colouring; one with the butterfly pea flower tea and the blue spirulina powder; and one with the lemon-lime tea and the yellow food colouring.

Bake the cakes until their edges start to brown and pull away from the edges of the cake tins. The cakes are done when a skewer inserted in the centre of each one comes out clean, 30–35 minutes.

Remove from the oven and set aside to cool in their tins, about 1 hour.

When the cakes are cool, layer them on a serving platter, placing 100g jam between each cake.

TO MAKE THE ICING

In a medium bowl, combine the icing sugar and milk until well combined and a smooth and silky icing forms, about 7 minutes. Drizzle the icing over the top of the cake, allowing it to go over the edges of the cake.

Scatter the top of the cake with edible gold dust and tiny stars.

Store at room temperature in an airtight container for 2–3 days.

✦ MUGGLE MAGIC ✦

Although the numerical name is appropriate for the four houses, *petits fours* actually means 'small oven'. And that too is a misnomer as these colourful pastries are not cooked in small ovens! The 'small' in the name refers to the low heat used to bake these treats.

YIELD: 10 SCONES

DOLORES UMBRIDGE'S I WILL MAKE SCONES

As Harry Potter serves a late afternoon detention in Dolores Umbridge's office in Harry Potter and the Order of the Phoenix, the professor drinks the traditional teatime cup of tea (filled with spoonfuls of pink sugar). Surprisingly, Umbridge does not accompany the drink with one of the most popular pastries typically served at an afternoon tea: crumbly, dense and lightly sweet scones.

Umbridge is far from sweet. 'I think she's a monster and to be played as such,' says Imelda Staunton. 'I don't need to understand what she does, but from a character point of view, she believes she's doing the absolute best for that school.'

Scones are the perfect confection to complement your teatime, and this recipe yields gilded, raised rounds of deliciousness. If Umbridge had accompanied her tea with something sweet, these scones would be the absolute best.

250g flour, plus extra for dusting

1 tablespoon baking powder

5 teaspoons sugar

1 teaspoon salt

75g dried currants

200ml double cream

FOR THE TOPPING

1 egg white, lightly beaten with 1 teaspoon water

Preheat the oven to 220°C/200°C fan/Gas Mark 7. Have at hand an ungreased large baking tray.

In a large bowl, whisk together the flour, baking powder, 2 teaspoons of the sugar and the salt. Using a large spoon, stir in the currants and cream just until combined. Using your hands, gently gather the mixture together, kneading it against the side of the bowl until it holds together in a rough ball.

Lightly flour a work surface and turn the dough out on to it. Roll out the dough about 2cm thick. Using a 7.5cm round cutter, cut out rounds from the dough, pressing straight down and lifting straight up and spacing them as closely together as possible. Place the dough rounds at least 5cm apart on the baking tray. Gather up the dough trimmings, knead briefly on the floured work surface, roll out the dough again, cut out more rounds and add them to the tray.

Using a pastry brush, lightly brush the tops of the scones with the egg white mixture, then scatter evenly with the remaining 3 teaspoons of sugar.

Bake the scones until golden, 10–12 minutes. Transfer to a wire rack to cool. Serve warm or at room temperature.

✦ BEHIND THE MAGIC ✦

Imelda Staunton describes Dolores Umbridge as 'madness and cruelty dressed up. I'm not just a lady in a very nice array of pink outfits.'

V ✦ YIELD: 20–25 MINI SANDWICHES

TEDDY THE NIFFLER'S TWO-BITE GOLD COIN SANDWICH CAKES

Even though Teddy the Niffler may be Eddie Redmayne's favourite beast in the Fantastic Beasts films, the actor describes this crafty animal as the bane of his character's existence. Nifflers are attracted to shiny objects and will go to any length to obtain them. In *Fantastic Beasts and Where to Find Them*, Teddy even squeezes into a bank security vault and stuffs his pouch with gold from the deposit boxes – something Newt cannot allow! The Magizoologist needs to relieve the Niffler of the sparkling, glittering objects he's collected.

During his research for the part, Redmayne spent time with a zoologist who worked with a baby anteater. 'It would curl up into a little ball, and in order to make it relax, she would tickle his little belly,' says Redmayne. So, in order to make Teddy release the gold and other glittering objects he has acquired, Newt tickles him.

Every Niffler would be attracted to these lemon-flavoured cakes filled with a buttery filling and sprayed with edible gold lustre dust.

FOR THE SANDWICH CAKES

- 250g plain flour
- 1¼ teaspoons bicarbonate of soda
- ¼ teaspoon salt
- 200g granulated sugar
- 115g butter
- 1½ teaspoons vanilla extract
- 1 medium egg, at room temperature
- Juice and zest from 1 lemon
- 1 teaspoon yellow food colouring
- 175ml full-fat milk

FOR THE FILLING

- 750g icing sugar
- 335g butter, softened
- 1 tablespoon vanilla extract
- 75ml full-fat milk
- 1 tablespoon edible gold sprinkles

FOR THE GARNISH

- 100g edible gold lustre dust and star-shaped sprinkles

> 'FOR THE LAST TIME, YOU PILFERINGGPEST – PAWS OFF WHAT DOESN'T BELONG TO YOU!'
>
> – Newt Scamander
> *Fantastic Beasts and Where to Find Them*

TO MAKE THE SANDWICH CAKES

Preheat the oven to 180°C/160°C fan/Gas Mark 4. Line a baking sheet with baking paper.

In a large bowl, combine the flour, bicarbonate of soda and salt until well blended. Set aside.

In the bowl of a stand mixer or a large bowl with a hand mixer on a high speed, beat together the sugar and butter until light, fluffy and well blended. Mix in the vanilla, egg, lemon juice and zest (reserving ⅓ of the zest to scatter on top), and the food colouring; combine well.

Beat in half of the flour mixture, followed by half of the milk. Repeat until everything is incorporated and blended well.

Use an ice-cream scoop to create balls with the dough. Place the balls of dough 5cm apart on the prepared baking sheet. Bake until firm and a little bit browned around the edges, 10–15 minutes. Remove from the oven and set aside to cool.

TO MAKE THE FILLING

In the bowl of a stand mixer or a large mixing bowl with a hand mixer, combine the icing sugar, butter, vanilla and milk. Mix on a medium speed until combined thoroughly and the icing is thick yet spreadable, about 10 minutes.

When the cakes have cooled, assemble the sandwiches: spread icing on the base cake, and place another cake on top of the icing. Spread the edible gold hundreds and thousands on a plate. Before the icing dries, roll each of the sandwich cakes in the plate of sprinkles so that they are all around each of the sandwiches. Scatter some of the edible gold lustre dust and star-shaped sprinkles on top of each sandwich; scatter the remaining ⅓ of lemon zest on top for extra flavour and decoration.

Store at room temperature in an airtight container for 2–3 days.

'HEY, KNOCK IT OFF.'

– Queenie Goldstein to a hovering teapot who won't stop nudging her for more tea

Fantastic Beasts: The Crimes of Grindelwald

GF, V ✦ YIELD: 12 SERVINGS

QUEENIE GOLDSTEIN'S FLOATING TEAPOT

Queenie Goldstein finds herself alone and lost in Paris, unable to find her sister, Tina, in *Fantastic Beasts: The Crimes of Grindelwald*. She is 'befriended' by Vinda Rosier, an acolyte of Gellert Grindelwald. At their chateau, Vinda tries to persuade Queenie to join their cause and offers her tea from a floating teapot. Queenie is not convinced and wants to leave, but the teapot keeps hovering in mid-air, nudging her, intent on refilling her cup.

This dish takes teatime to a new level, with its own floating teapot, creating an enchanting centrepiece for presenting sweeteners for your tea, including honey, bright pink sugar hearts and crystallised ginger. There are also other tea condiments: lemon, milk and mint. To cut little sprigs of fresh mint for the tea, a pair of manicure scissors hangs on a ribbon from the teapot! If your teapot isn't ready in (tea) time, you can circle the sweeteners and condiments around a non-floating teapot.

FOR THE CRYSTALLISED GINGER

100g fresh gingerroot, peeled and chopped into 1cm pieces

400g granulated sugar

FOR THE SUGAR HEARTS

1 cup bright pink coarse sugar

SPECIALIST TOOLS

2.5cm heart-shaped silicone mould

TO MAKE THE CRYSTALLISED GINGER

Place the gingerroot, 500ml water and 200g of the sugar in a saucepan over a high heat and bring to the boil. Reduce the heat to medium and simmer for 1 hour.

Remove the gingerroot and strain it. Discard the sugar water. In a small mixing bowl, toss the gingerroot in the remaining 200g of sugar. Set aside to dry and cool, about 30 minutes. Remove the ginger pieces from the sugar and place them in a serving dish.

TO MAKE THE SUGAR HEARTS

In a medium mixing bowl, combine the pink sugar and 1 teaspoon of water until all of the sugar is somewhat moistened and reaches a tacky consistency, about 1 minute. Pack 2–3 pinches of the mixture into a 2.5cm heart-shaped silicone mould. Pack the sugar in evenly and firmly, ensuring there are no open pockets in the mould.

Cover a work surface with a sheet of greaseproof paper. Push the sugar hearts out of the moulds and on to the greaseproof paper. Allow the hearts to rest until firm, about 30 minutes. For best results, cover the hearts with another sheet of greaseproof paper, and allow to sit for 4–6 hours or overnight. Transfer a small serving bowl.

CONTINUED ON PAGE 72

CONTINUED FROM PAGE 71

FOR THE FLOATING TEAPOT CENTREPIECE

500g bottle of a very strong waterproof polyurethane adhesive

1 tea tray

1 teacup and saucer

One 30cm metal barspoon

1 small teapot, preferably a silver pot with an attached lid

1 large bunch fresh mint

One 30cm piece thin ribbon

1 pair of manicure scissors

1 large lemon, cut into thin slices, quartered

600g honey

5 clear glass bowls or teacups

1 set of sugar cube tongs

NOTE ✦ If you do not have a mould, use your fingers to roll the sugar into tiny balls.

TO MAKE THE FLOATING TEAPOT CENTREPIECE

Apply 2 tablespoons of the polyurethane adhesive on the tea tray where the tea saucer will be placed. Set the saucer on top of the adhesive. Apply 1 tablespoon of the polyurethane adhesive to the top of the saucer, and set the teacup on top of the polyurethane adhesive. Allow it to sit until the polyurethane adhesive hardens, about 4 hours. Place a heavy object on top to help secure the items as they set and the adhesive dries.

Bend the barspoon up on an angle at the base, and down on an angle at the top, so that the spoon is curved on both ends in a shape that will fit along the side of the inside of the teacup and into the spout of the teapot.

Fill the teacup ⅓ full with the polyurethane adhesive, and place the round end of the spoon in the polyurethane adhesive. Place something alongside the spoon to support it while the polyurethane adhesive hardens. Allow it to sit until it hardens, at least 4 hours, but preferably overnight.

When the polyurethane adhesive has hardened and the barspoon is secure, lay the tea tray on its side, using towels to prop up spots that don't reach the table, and put the top of the barspoon into the spout of the teapot. Generously apply the polyurethane adhesive to secure the top of the barspoon inside the spout of the teapot. Let the adhesive harden for 24–48 hours.

When it is time to serve, cover the spots where there is hardened polyurethane adhesive with clingfilm. Fill the teapot and teacup with fresh mint, and wrap fresh mint around the barspoon so that it is no longer visible. Be sure that the mint does not come in contact with the hardened polyurethane adhesive. Use the ribbon to tie the manicure scissors to the teapot for guests to use to clip bits of fresh mint for their tea.

Place the lemon, honey, crystallised ginger and sugar hearts each in separate clear glass bowls. Set the sugar cube tongs in the dish with the sugar hearts.

Store the candied ginger, lemon and fresh mint in the refrigerator in separate airtight containers for 1–2 days. Store the sugar hearts at room temperature in an airtight container for 3–4 weeks.

CHAPTER TWO

SAVOURY TEATIME FINGER FOODS

GF, V ✦ YIELD: 16 SERVINGS

DURMSTRANG INSTITUTE SHOPSKA SALAD TEA PARTY BOATS

Shopska salad is the Bulgarian national salad, and its ingredients evoke the colours of the Bulgarian flag with rich, red diced tomatoes, green cucumbers and parsley, and white from onions and *tvorog* (farmer cheese). The classic Eastern European salad here is served in bite-sized chicory leaves that evoke Durmstrang's ship.

For his part as Durmstrang champion, Stanislav Ianevski (Durmstrang champion Viktor Krum) learnt how to scuba dive for the second task of the Triwizard Tournament, which takes place under the Black Lake. He also learnt how to dive from a platform for a scene where Viktor jumps off the Durmstrang ship, but unfortunately the scene did not make it to the final cut of the film.

FOR THE SHOPSKA SALAD

- 6 large vine-ripened tomatoes, diced
- 2 large cucumbers, skin on, sliced into tiny wedges
- 1 large poblano pepper, trimmed, deseeded and diced
- 1 large bunch parsley, chopped stalks removed
- 80g red onion, diced
- 300g feta cheese

TO MAKE THE SHOPSKA SALAD

In a large mixing bowl, combine the tomatoes, cucumbers, poblano, parsley, onion and feta cheese. Set aside.

TO MAKE THE DRESSING

Use a grater to zest the oranges into a large mixing bowl and set aside. Cut the oranges in half, and squeeze the juice of the oranges into a salad dressing shaker. Add the honey, champagne vinegar, olive oil, garlic, salt and pepper, and shake until combined well and the consistency of the dressing becomes milky. In place of a salad shaker, use a large mixing spoon to stir the ingredients together in a large mixing bowl.

Pour the dressing over the salad, and mix until the dressing thoroughly coats the salad.

CONTINUED ON PAGE 78

CONTINUED FROM PAGE 77

FOR THE DRESSING

2 medium oranges

4 tablespoons honey

1 tablespoon champagne vinegar

2 tablespoons extra-virgin olive oil

2 garlic cloves, very finely chopped

1 pinch pink Himalayan sea salt

1 pinch freshly ground multicoloured pepper

FOR PRESENTING THE SALAD

1 head radicchio

4 heads Belgian endive

NOTE ✦ If you cannot find an imported Bulgarian *tvorog* cheese, also known as white brine *sirene*, any Greek feta cheese will do.

Cover a serving platter one-layer-deep with radicchio leaves; arrange the chicory leaves on top. Try to use the chicory leaves that are in the best condition. Fill each leaf with the salad, making sure that each of the ingredients are in each of the leaves.

Garnish with the orange zest.

Store in the refrigerator in an airtight container for 1–2 days.

> 'AND NOW OUR FRIENDS FROM THE NORTH – PLEASE GREET THE PROUD SONS OF DURMSTRANG.'
>
> – Albus Dumbledore
>
> *Harry Potter and the Goblet of Fire*

GF✤ ✦ YIELD: 12 SERVINGS

MINI FRIED RAVEN EGG TEA SANDWICHES

During his time at Hogwarts, seen in *Fantastic Beasts: The Crimes of Grindelwald*, shy, focused Hufflepuff Newt Scamander befriends the troubled, aristocratic Slytherin Leta Lestrange. Looking for a place to hide after a particularly bad incident, Leta stumbles upon a tower sanctuary where Newt tends to helpless beasts – including a newly hatched raven chick.

'It's their oddness that brings them together,' says Zoë Kravitz (Leta). 'Newt is such a compassionate person. He loves the things that no one else will love, and Leta is that in a lot of ways. He sees this sad beast, or as Leta would say, a monster, in her and loves that about her, doesn't want to change a thing about her.'

These two-bite tea sandwiches are made with eggs – chicken, not raven! – fried 'over easy' and scattered with cheddar cheese and pepper. They're served on quarters of toasted bread, and then scattered with a hot Hungarian paprika inspired by Leta's tempestuous nature.

- 6 large slices wheat rye bread
- 30g butter
- 12 medium eggs
- ¼ teaspoon salt
- ¼ teaspoon freshly ground pepper
- 2 tablespoons grated cheddar cheese
- 1 pinch hot Hungarian paprika

NOTE ✦ For a gluten-free savoury teatime treat, serve the fried eggs without the bread or with your favourite gluten-free bread.

Toast the bread, and cut the crusts from around the edges of each slice. Cut each slice into quarters.

In a frying pan over a medium heat, melt the butter.

Fry the eggs until the yolks are solid but still soft, about 2 minutes on each side. Season the eggs with the salt and pepper, and scatter over the cheese.

Use a slotted turner to separate the eggs so that there are 12 cooked eggs, each with a yolk.

Place an egg on top of each of the toast quarters, removing the white edges or flipping them over on top, to make each egg fit on the toast quarter. Top each egg with another quarter. Secure each sandwich with a bamboo cocktail stick.

Arrange the sandwiches on a platter to serve. Scatter the tops of the sandwiches with the hot Hungarian paprika.

Store the eggs in the refrigerator in an airtight container for 2–3 days. Store the bread at room temperature in an airtight container for 3–4 days.

SALADE NIÇOISE TEATIME BOAT BITES

GF ✦ YIELD: 16 SERVINGS

After they debark the Hogwarts Express, first-year students are ferried across the Black Lake before arriving at the Great Hall. Alfred Enoch, who plays Gryffindor Dean Thomas, says he will never forget the experience of crossing the lake in the small, lantern-lit boats. The film-makers had built a shallow, but vast, tank in the studio, with metal pulleys that 'sailed' the boats. 'When I saw it in the cinema, it seemed so effortless,' he remembers. 'That was one of the first times I saw what was behind the magic, as it were. Although it gives an appearance of absolute smoothness, putting these things together isn't effortless, and I appreciated the hard work and craftsmanship that happens behind it.'

Inspired by these boats in *Harry Potter and the Philosopher's Stone*, these individual two-bite servings of radicchio leaves are filled with lemony baked tuna, roasted potatoes, green beans, hard-boiled egg, tomato and salty kalamata olives, bathed in a light, tangy Dijon mustard dressing that will really float your boat!

FOR THE TUNA

45g butter, softened

2 x 225g tuna steaks

1 lemon

¼ teaspoon salt

¼ teaspoon freshly ground pepper

25g fresh dill, chopped

FOR THE ROASTED BABY POTATOES

15g butter

150g baby potatoes, chopped into 1cm square pieces

1 garlic clove, very finely chopped

¼ teaspoon pink Himalayan sea salt

¼ teaspoon freshly ground multicoloured pepper

FOR THE SALAD

3 medium eggs, hard-boiled and chopped into 1cm square pieces

2 medium vine-ripened tomatoes, chopped into 1cm square pieces

50g green beans, chopped into 1cm pieces

25g pitted kalamata olives, chopped into 1cm pieces

1 head radicchio

FOR THE SALAD DRESSING

125g Dijon mustard

2 tablespoons champagne vinegar

Juice of 1 lemon

1 garlic clove, very finely chopped

¼ teaspoon salt

¼ teaspoon freshly ground black pepper

¼ teaspoon sugar

TO MAKE THE TUNA

Preheat the oven to 190°C/170°C fan/Gas Mark 5. Use 15g of butter to grease the inside of a flan tin or a 20cm square baking dish.

Rinse the tuna steaks, and put them in the dish. Cut the lemon in half, and cut one half of the lemon into thin slices. Squeeze the other lemon half over the tuna, and place a half of a thin slice of lemon on top of each tuna steak. Place 15g of butter on top of each tuna steak; season each tuna steak with the salt and pepper and scatter with half the dill.

Bake the tuna until it flakes easily with a fork, about 30 minutes. The internal temperature should be 51.6°C.

Set the tuna aside for a few minutes to cool, then place in the refrigerator.

Leave the oven on at 190°C/170°C fan/Gas Mark 5 to roast the potatoes.

TO MAKE THE ROASTED BABY POTATOES

Use the butter to grease a flan tin or a 20cm square baking dish, and place the potatoes in the dish. Toss the potatoes with the garlic and season with salt and pepper.

Roast the potatoes in the oven until golden brown and a little crispy around the edges, 10–12 minutes, stirring after 8 minutes. Set aside to cool to room temperature.

Flake the tuna steaks to make 1cm pieces.

TO MAKE THE SALAD

In a large bowl, combine the potatoes, eggs, tomatoes, beans and olives.

TO MAKE THE SALAD DRESSING

In a salad dressing shaker, combine the mustard, champagne vinegar, lemon juice, garlic, salt, pepper and sugar, and shake until blended together thoroughly, about 20 revolutions. In place of a salad shaker, use a large mixing spoon to stir the ingredients together for 30 revolutions in a large mixing bowl.

Add the dressing to the salad, and gently stir to ensure that the dressing coats all of the ingredients well. Add the tuna and lightly fold in, turning only 2–3 times so that the tuna does not shred.

Pick out 16 of the sturdiest, smallest radicchio leaves. Fill each of the leaves with the salad, ensuring that each of the ingredients is in each of the leaves. Arrange the leaves on a platter, scatter the remaining fresh chopped dill on top and serve.

Store in the refrigerator in an airtight container for 2–3 days.

'RIGHT THEN! FIRST-YEARS! THIS WAY, PLEASE!'

– Rubeus Hagrid

Harry Potter and the Philosopher's Stone

YIELD: 12 SERVINGS

RON WEASLEY'S FINGER SANDWICH BITES

When the trolley witch comes around on the Hogwarts Express with a trolley filled with confections, Ron Weasley doesn't take her up on the offer – he's brought a sandwich from home, though he doesn't seem enthusiastic about it.

For the scene in the train coach, where Harry and Ron first meet, 'we were sitting opposite each other, and we were constantly giggling,' says Rupert Grint (Ron). 'We couldn't film it together, in fact, so we had to do it separately. [Director] Chris Columbus would play Harry's part when they were filming me, and then he would play me with Dan.'

This tasty dish is inspired by sandwiches Ron probably wished he'd had on the train: Tomato and Bacon, Egg Salad, and Devilled Ham. Arrange this variety of sandwiches on a platter, and garnish with cornichons, pickle slices or olives on sprigs of rosemary poked into the tops of a few of the sarnies.

TOMATO AND BACON SANDWICHES

225g bacon

2 vine-ripened tomatoes

1 teaspoon granulated sugar

4 slices caraway or rye bread

225g mayonnaise

4 tablespoons chiffonade fresh tarragon

1 teaspoon fresh lemon juice

¼ teaspoon pink Himalayan sea salt

¼ teaspoon freshly ground black pepper

¼ teaspoon hot Hungarian paprika

FOR GARNISH

Fresh thyme leaves

TO MAKE THE SANDWICHES

Preheat the oven to 180°C/160°C fan/Gas Mark 4. Spread the bacon rashers out flat on a baking sheet, and bake until crispy, about 30 minutes.

Remove the bacon from the oven and set the rashers on a plate lined with kitchen paper until they cool to room temperature.

Slice the tomatoes into 5mm-thick slices and scatter with the sugar.

TO MAKE THE SANDWICH SPREAD

In a food processor, combine the mayonnaise, tarragon, lemon juice, salt, pepper and paprika. Pulse everything together 3 times. Use a spoon to scrape the mixture from the sides of the food processor and pulse 2–3 more times until combined thoroughly.

Use a knife to remove the crusts from the bread slices. Smear some of the sandwich spread on a piece of bread. Place a thin slice of tomato on top, and place 3 rashers of crispy bacon on top of the tomato. Place a second piece of bread on top. Repeat to make a second sandwich. Cut the sandwiches down the middle both ways, creating quarters. Scatter fresh thyme leaves on top of the sandwiches.

CONTINUED ON PAGE 84

CONTINUED FROM PAGE 83

EGG SALAD SANDWICHES

4 eggs, hard-boiled

225g mayonnaise

60g mustard

¼ teaspoon pink Himalayan sea salt

¼ teaspoon freshly ground pepper

4 slices rye bread

1 tablespoon fresh thyme leaves

DEVILLED HAM SANDWICHES

225g ham, finely chopped

110g mayonnaise

2 tablespoons sweet pickle relish

1 tablespoon chopped celery

½ tablespoon diced red onion

¼ teaspoon freshly ground pepper

4 slices white bread

6–8 cornichons

6–8 sprigs fresh rosemary

TO MAKE EGG SALAD SANDWICHES

In a mixing bowl, use a masher to mash the eggs. Add the mayonnaise, mustard, salt and pepper, and mix to combine well.

Use a knife to remove the crusts from the bread slices, and cut each slice in half horizontally. Place the egg salad between the pieces of bread. Cut the sandwiches down the middle both ways, creating quarters. Scatter fresh thyme leaves on top of the sandwiches.

TO MAKE DEVILLED HAM SANDWICHES

In a mixing bowl, combine the ham, mayonnaise, pickle relish, celery, onion and pepper.

Use a knife to remove the crusts from the bread slices, and cut each slice in half. Place the ham salad between the pieces of bread. Cut the sandwiches down the middle both ways, creating quarters. Top each sandwich with a cornichon on a sprig of rosemary.

Store the sandwich fillings in the refrigerator in separate airtight containers for 2–3 days. Store the breads at room temperature in airtight containers for 4–5 days.

'ANYTHING OFF THE TROLLEY, DEARS?'

'NO, THANKS. I'M ALL SET.'

– Trolley Witch and Ron Weasley
Harry Potter and the Philosopher's Stone

LEAKY CAULDRON SPLIT PEA TEATIME SOUP

GF ✦ YIELD: 12 SERVINGS

Harry Potter is first taken to the wizarding world's most popular pub and inn, the Leaky Cauldron, by Hagrid in *Harry Potter and the Philosopher's Stone*, where he learns he is The Boy Who Lived. In *Harry Potter and the Prisoner of Azkaban*, after storming out of Privet Drive, he takes the Knight Bus to the Leaky Cauldron, where he meets with Minister for Magic Cornelius Fudge. Fudge offers him pea soup, which Harry declines – he's been warned about it by Dre Head, the shrunken head on the bus.

In developing a menu for the Leaky Cauldron for *Philosopher's Stone*, the graphics department included a cauldron full of potential soup entrées, posted on a sign in the tavern, including Leaky House Soup; House Soup Leaky; Leaky, Leaky Soup; and Soup, Soup, Soup.

This soup won't eat you and is in fact a classic split pea soup made with split peas, carrots, celery, onions and ham. Serve it warm, in individual teacups, clear coupe glasses or ceramic ramekins.

- 450g dried green split peas
- 1 ham bone with plenty of meat on it
- 1 medium or large red or brown onion, chopped
- 1 teaspoon salt
- ½ teaspoon pepper
- 4 bay leaves
- 10 sticks carrots, chopped into 5 pence-sized pieces
- 5 sticks celery, chopped into 5 pence-sized pieces

Using a sieve, rinse the peas in cold water and let drain for a few minutes. In a large saucepan or casserole over a high heat, cover the peas with 5cm of water. Boil for 3 minutes, and then take off heat and let soak for up to 8 hours (or overnight). Using a sieve, rinse the peas and then drain.

In a large saucepan or casserole over a high heat, place the peas, 2 litres of water, the ham bone, onion, salt, pepper and bay leaves. Bring to the boil and then reduce the heat to medium and simmer for 90 minutes, stirring occasionally.

Take out the ham bone and remove the meat. Dice the meat and return it to the pot. Add the carrots and celery. Continue to simmer for about 1 hour or until the peas and water are no longer separate. Stir throughout.

Serve in clear coupe glasses or, for a smaller option, in clear glass shot glasses.

Store in the refrigerator in an airtight container for 3–4 days.

> 'IF YOU HAVE PEA SOUP, MAKE SURE YOU EAT IT BEFORE IT EATS YOU.'
>
> – Dre Head to Harry Potter
>
> *Harry Potter and the Prisoner of Azkaban*

'PULL YOURSELF TOGETHER, MAN.
YOU'RE GOING INTO THE FOREST!'

– Argus Filch to Rubeus Hagrid

*Harry Potter and
the Philosopher's Stone*

FORBIDDEN FOREST MINI MUSHROOM STRUDELS

V ✦ YIELD: 8 SERVINGS

The Forbidden Forest appeared in each Harry Potter film, with the exception of *Harry Potter and the Deathly Hallows – Part 1* (though Harry, Ron and Hermione spend time in several other forests). The massive, mist-filled Forbidden Forest became more theatrical and more frightening each time it was entered. For *Harry Potter and the Order of the Phoenix*, production designer Stuart Craig redesigned the trees' roots after tropical mangrove trees, which looked to him as though the trunks were supported by fingers.

These bite-sized savoury strudels, stuffed with mushrooms, which have been fried in white wine, red onion, thyme and garlic, offer a very earthy dish inspired by the plant life that would be prevalent along the base of the trees in the mysterious forest.

- 450g puff pastry, thawed if frozen
- 60g butter, softened
- 275g mushrooms, sliced
- 125ml dry white wine
- 4 teaspoons fresh thyme leaves
- 1 tablespoon diced red onion
- 1 garlic clove, very finely chopped
- 1 egg white

Preheat the oven to 180°C/160°C fan/Gas Mark 4. Line a 23 x 30cm baking sheet with baking paper.

In a large frying pan over a high heat, melt 30g of butter. Add the mushrooms, wine, 3 teaspoons of the thyme, the onion and garlic. Bring to a boil, then reduce the heat to medium and simmer until the wine is cooked out, 20–25 minutes.

Remove from the heat, and set aside to cool.

Cut the pastry into eight 10 x 5cm rectangles and twenty-four 5mm-thick strips that are 10cm long. Create 8 plaits, one for each strudel: Using three strips side by side, cross the left strip over the centre strip, then cross the right strip over the centre strip, alternating, until the full length of each strip is plaited.

CONTINUED ON PAGE 88

✦ BEHIND THE MAGIC ✦

The biggest forest was built for *Harry Potter and the Deathly Hallows – Part 2*, where a cyclorama backdrop circling the set was over 180 metres in length.

CONTINUED FROM PAGE 87

When the mushroom mixture is cool, place 3 tablespoons of the mixture on one side of each rectangular piece of pastry. Leave a 1cm border around the sides. Place ¼ teaspoon butter on top of the mushroom mixture on each piece of pastry. Fold the other side of each piece of pastry over the mushroom mixture. Use the tines of a fork to press down the dough together on the three sides where the top and base come together.

Place one pastry plait on one of the long sides of each of the strudels; press down the top of the plait in the top corner of the strudel to secure the plait. The plait will extend over the base edge of the pastry by 1cm.

Lightly beat the egg white, and use a pastry brush to cover each strudel with the egg white.

Pierce the top of each strudel with a knife to create ventilation. Place the strudels on the prepared baking sheet. Bake until golden brown and flaky, 35–40 minutes.

Garnish with the remaining 1 teaspoon fresh thyme.

Store in the refrigerator in an airtight container for 2–3 days.

LUNA LOVEGOOD'S HONEY-ROASTED RADISH SALAD

GF, V ✦ YIELD: 4 SERVINGS

Growing outside the Lovegood house are orange-coloured floating Dirigible Plum bushes that must have compelled daughter Luna into creating a pair of earrings based on the fruit, as seen in *Harry Potter and the Order of the Phoenix*. However, when costume designer Jany Temime first assigned the earrings to a crafter to construct, they arrived in the shape of red radishes. Actress Evanna Lynch (Luna), a well-informed Harry Potter fan, advised Temime that the earrings needed to be refashioned to match the fruit – in fact, Lynch crafted her proper earrings herself, seen on screen.

This warm teatime salad of colourful roasted radishes and herbs gives a great dose of potassium and vitamin C in this pretty and flavourful side salad. The dish can be served either as a salad to pass around, or individually to each guest in a clear glass dish, wine glass or champagne flute, to show the pretty colours of the radishes.

FOR THE RADISHES

- 35–40 mix-coloured radishes
- 2 garlic cloves, very finely chopped
- 1 tablespoon honey

FOR THE DRESSING

- 1 tablespoon champagne vinegar
- ½ tablespoon extra-virgin olive oil
- ¼ teaspoon freshly ground black pepper
- 1 pinch salt
- 1 pinch granulated sugar

TO MAKE THE RADISHES

Preheat the oven to 180°C/160°C fan/Gas Mark 4. Line a baking sheet with baking paper.

Clean and trim the radishes; cut the large radishes in half. Chiffonade some of the radish leaves.

In a large mixing bowl, lightly toss the radishes with the garlic and honey.

Arrange the radishes and some of the leaves (reserve 2 leaves, chiffonade, for garnish) on the prepared baking sheet. Bake until the edges of the radishes start to turn a light brown colour, 15–20 minutes.

Remove from the oven and set aside to cool.

TO MAKE THE DRESSING

Combine the champagne vinegar, olive oil, pepper, salt and sugar in a salad shaker, and shake for 20 revolutions. In place of a salad shaker, use a large mixing spoon to stir the ingredients well in a large mixing bowl.

When the radishes have cooled, pour the dressing over them in a large mixing bowl and lightly toss. Arrange the radish salad on a plate. Lightly scatter some of the chiffonade fresh radish leaves on top for colour.

Store in the refrigerator in an airtight container for 3–4 days, but it's best if eaten immediately while fresh and warm.

'KEEP OFF THE DIRIGIBLE PLUMS'

– Sign outside the Lovegood house

Harry Potter and the Deathly Hallows – Part 1

GF ✦ YIELD: 4 SERVINGS

BLACK LAKE COD CAKES WITH POACHED EGGS AND BRANDY CREAM SAUCE

During the second task of the Triwizard Tournament in *Harry Potter and the Goblet of Fire*, Harry encounters the merpeople that live in the waters of the Black Lake. These underwater creatures are far from what Muggles call a mermaid. They are, as creature designer Nick Dudman describes them, nothing to tangle with.

The merpeople animators melded the creature's fish and human characteristics instead of presenting them as a human with a fish tail. Basing the design on a sturgeon, they added sea anemone–like hair, and a scythe-like fish tail that moves side to side, like a typical fish, instead of up and down.

These cod cakes offer another engaging combination by covering each with a soft poached egg topped with a brandy cream sauce flavoured with paprika, multicoloured peppercorns and red chilli flakes. Serve these on small plates arranged on a table or a side buffet.

FOR THE COD CAKES

15g butter

2 fillets cod or haddock (about 450g)

Juice from 1 lemon

¼ teaspoon salt

¼ teaspoon freshly ground black pepper

75g crackers, crushed

60g fresh parsley, chopped

2 medium eggs

2 tablespoons finely chopped red onion

1 small garlic clove, very finely chopped

1 teaspoon mustard powder

4 tablespoons full-fat milk

FOR THE BRANDY CREAM SAUCE

500ml double cream

2 tablespoons brandy

¼ teaspoon red chilli flakes

1 pinch pink Himalayan sea salt

1 pinch freshly ground multicoloured pepper

4 tablespoons paprika

FOR THE POACHED EGGS

1 teaspoon vinegar

4 medium eggs

FOR THE GARNISH

1 large lemon, cut into 1cm wedges

> 'MYRTLE... THERE AREN'T MEEPEOPLE IN THE BLACK LAKE, ARE THERE?'
>
> – Harry Potter to Moaning Myrtle
>
> *Harry Potter and the Goblet of Fire*

TO MAKE THE COD CAKES

Preheat the oven to 180°C/160°C fan/Gas Mark 4. Use 1 teaspoon of butter to grease a 20cm square baking dish or a flan tin.

Rinse the fish fillets in cold water. Place the fish fillets in the prepared baking dish. Squeeze the juice of half of the lemon over the fish; season with salt and pepper, and lay 1 teaspoon of butter on top of each filet.

Bake the fish until lightly browned around the edges and starting to pull away from the baking dish around the edges, 30–40 minutes. Remove from the oven and set aside until cool enough to handle, about 5 minutes. Leave the oven on.

Using a fork, flake the fish. In a large mixing bowl, use your hands to combine the fish with the crushed crackers, 45g of the parsley, the eggs, the other half of the lemon juice, the onion, garlic, mustard powder and milk until the mixture becomes a consistency that can be formed into 4 round fishcakes. Each fishcake should be about 7.5cm round and 1cm high.

In a separate large baking dish, bake the fishcakes until the edges are golden brown and start to pull away from the baking dish, 30–40 minutes. Remove them from the oven and set aside until assembly.

TO MAKE THE BRANDY CREAM SAUCE

In a medium saucepan over a high heat, bring the cream to the boil. Reduce the heat to medium-high and stir occasionally as it continues to cook and thicken, about 10 minutes. Add the brandy, red chilli flakes, salt, pepper and 3½ tablespoons paprika. Stir well to combine. Continue cooking until the sauce thickens, 25–30 minutes.

TO MAKE THE POACHED EGGS

Fill a large saucepan with 1.5 litres of water over a high heat. Bring the water to the boil, then reduce the heat to medium. As the water simmers, add the vinegar and stir until combined well. Gently crack an egg into the water and let it poach until it becomes solid but the yolk looks like it would still run if released, 2–3 minutes. Poach the eggs one at a time for the best results. Using two large mixing spoons, delicately remove each egg when it is poached, setting each one on a plate on the side.

Place a fishcake on each plate. Pour ¼ of the sauce over each fishcake. Carefully place a poached egg on top of each fishcake. Garnish with the remaining parsley, lemon wedges and a scattering of the remaining ½ tablespoon paprika on top.

Store the fishcakes, sauce and eggs in the refrigerator in separate airtight containers for 1–2 days, but they're best if eaten immediately when freshly made.

DEATHLY HALLOWS PULL-APART TEATIME BREAD

V ✦ YIELD: 12 SERVINGS

When prop makers originally designed the Resurrection Stone for *Harry Potter and the Half-Blood Prince*, they were unaware the Deathly Hallows should be etched upon it. Luckily, the seventh book came out before the design was finished, establishing the symbol.

This unique bread evokes the three components of the sign of the Deathly Hallows: mini cheesy pull-apart breads with a hint of onion are arranged in the shape of a triangle, referencing the Cloak of Invisibility. The straight line of the Elder Wand is created with fresh thyme and rosemary. And the circle for the Resurrection Stone is formed by a tomato dipping sauce served in a round dish in the centre.

The bread is served in individual portions, with a serving for each guest formed in a triangle shape. This serving arrangement is similar to pull-apart buns, except these teatime bites are savoury. This can be presented on a tea tray by itself, either on the table or on a side buffet.

FOR THE PULL-APART BREAD TRIANGLE

- 675g unbaked croissants or puff pastry sheets, thawed if frozen
- 150g mini mozzarella cheese balls (pearls)
- 50g grated Parmesan cheese
- 115g butter, melted
- 1 tablespoon diced red onion
- 1 teaspoon chopped fresh rosemary
- 1 tablespoon chopped fresh oregano leaves
- ¼ teaspoon salt
- ¼ teaspoon freshly ground black pepper
- 1 egg white

TO MAKE THE PULL-APART BREAD TRIANLE

Preheat the oven to 180°C/160°C fan/Gas Mark 4. Line a 23 x 30cm baking sheet with baking paper.

Cut the dough into 2.5cm pieces and place in a large bowl. Add the mozzarella, Parmesan cheese, butter, onion, rosemary, oregano, salt and pepper, and stir 3–4 times until combined well and the pieces of dough are covered in the melted butter thoroughly.

Arrange the dough mixture on the prepared baking sheet in the outline of a large triangle. Beat the egg white lightly in a small bowl, and use a pastry brush to cover the bread with the egg white.

Bake until golden brown all around, especially around the edges, about 45 minutes. Remove from the oven and place the bread on a cheese board, chopping board or large platter. Leave the oven on.

CONTINUED ON PAGE 96

CONTINUED FROM PAGE 95

FOR THE TOMATO SAUCE

8 large vine-ripened tomatoes, chopped into 2.5cm pieces

125g tomato purée

125ml extra-virgin olive oil

15g fresh oregano leaves, chopped

½ teaspoon finely chopped rosemary

2 garlic cloves, very finely chopped

1 teaspoon granulated sugar

¼ teaspoon pink Himalayan sea salt

¼ teaspoon freshly ground multicoloured pepper

FOR THE GARNISH

2 long sprigs fresh rosemary

1 tablespoon grated Parmesan cheese

1 teaspoon finely chopped fresh rosemary

1 teaspoon chopped fresh oregano leaves

¼ teaspoon red chilli flakes

TO MAKE THE TOMATO SAUCE

In a large bowl, combine the tomatoes, tomato purée, oil, oregano, rosemary, garlic, sugar, salt and pepper. Stir 3–4 times until blended well and coated in the oil.

Place the mixture into a roasting pan, and roast until the skins have loosened from the tomatoes, about 45 minutes. Stir after 30 minutes.

Remove from the oven, and use a spoon to mash down the tomatoes and stir everything several times.

Place a round clear glass dish in the middle of the bread triangle on the cheese board and fill it with the tomato sauce for dipping the bread. Place a long sprig of rosemary in a vertical line over the tomato sauce, ensuring that the rosemary extends from the top to the base of the bread triangle, in the centre. Garnish by scattering with the Parmesan cheese, rosemary, oregano and red chilli flakes.

Store the tomato sauce in the refrigerator in an airtight container for 2–3 days. Store the bread at room temperature in an airtight container for 2–3 days.

'THE ELDER WAND. THE RESURRECTION STONE. THE CLOAK OF INVISIBILITY. TOGETHER, THEY MAKE UP THE DEATHLY HALLOWS. TOGETHER, THEY MAKE ONE THE MASTER OF DEATH.'

– Xenophilius Lovegood

Harry Potter and the Deathly Hallows – Part 1

GF ✦ YIELD: 8 SERVINGS

GREAT HALL TREACLE AND PINOT NOIR-ROASTED TURKEY DRUMSTICKS

As Ron Weasley savours the welcome feast in the Great Hall during his first year at Hogwarts in *Harry Potter and the Philosopher's Stone*, he gobbles a pair of roasted drumsticks in two-handed style with gusto. Finishing those, he goes in for a third but is put off when Nearly Headless Nick's nearly headless head rises from the platter.

These turkey legs are basted with a hearty pinot noir wine heated with fresh sage, star anise, multicoloured peppercorns and a flavour Harry Potter adores – treacle!

The feasts served in the Great Hall throughout the Harry Potter films were 'catered' by the props department under the advisement of director Chris Columbus, who wanted to use real food. But as little food was actually eaten while filming, it became less and less inviting under the hot lights. After this, feast foods were typically created from moulded resin.

FOR THE DRUMSTICKS

- 4 tablespoons extra-virgin olive oil
- 8 turkey drumsticks
- ½ teaspoon pink Himalayan sea salt, divided
- ½ teaspoon freshly ground multicoloured pepper

TO MAKE THE DRUMSTICKS

Preheat the oven to 190°C/170°C fan/Gas Mark 5.

In a large frying pan over a medium heat, heat 2 tablespoons of the oil. Place the drumsticks in the frying pan, season with ¼ teaspoon each of salt and pepper, and colour them well on both sides, 8–10 minutes each side. Season with the remaining ¼ teaspoon of salt and ¼ teaspoon pepper after turning them over.

Grease a large roasting pan or casserole with the remaining 2 tablespoons oil. Place the cooked drumsticks in the greased pan.

CONTINUED ON PAGE 98

> 'I KNOW YOU. YOU'RE NEARLY HEADLESS NICK!'
>
> – Ron Weasley
>
> *Harry Potter and the Philosopher's Stone*

CONTINUED FROM PAGE 97

FOR THE BLACK TREACLE AND PINOT NOIR BASTE

- 250ml pinot noir wine
- 30g fresh sage, chopped
- 175g runny honey
- 55g brown sugar
- 85g treacle
- 1 teaspoon chopped ginger
- 2 garlic cloves, very finely chopped
- 1 bay leaf
- 1 star anise
- ½ teaspoon dried juniper berries
- ¼ teaspoon mustard powder
- ¼ teaspoon pink Himalayan sea salt
- ¼ teaspoon freshly ground multicoloured pepper
- 1 pinch ground cloves

TO MAKE THE BLACK TREACLE AND PINOT NOIR BASTE

In a small saucepan over a high heat, combine the wine, 15g of the sage, the honey, brown sugar, treacle, ginger, garlic, bay leaf, star anise, juniper berries, mustard, salt, pepper and clove. Bring to the boil. Reduce the heat to medium and simmer, stirring occasionally, for 45 minutes. Using a handheld fine-mesh sieve, strain the baste liquid into a large mixing bowl to remove the bay leaf, star anise and juniper berries.

Using a pastry brush, coat the drumsticks with a thick layer of the treacle and pinot noir baste.

Roast the drumsticks in the oven, uncovered, until the internal temperature of the meat is 74°C, 1 hour 30 minutes–2 hours. Flip the drumsticks after the first 45 minutes, and generously coat the top of the drumsticks with additional baste; repeat after 30 minutes more.

Arrange the drumsticks on a large platter, scatter with the remaining 15g of sage and serve.

Store in the refrigerator in an airtight container for 2–3 days.

BOWTRUCKLE ISLAND BUTTER BOARD

GF ✦ YIELD: 16 SERVINGS

As their friendship grows, Newt Scamander takes a forlorn Leta Lestrange to Bowtruckle Island on the Black Lake in order to cheer her up in *Fantastic Beasts: The Crimes of Grindelwald*. He shows her the family of Bowtruckles that live in a bushy-topped tree, shy but clever creatures with the appearance of a walking arrangement of twigs and leaves.

This particular butter board gives tribute to Bowtruckle Island's inhabitants with florets of broccoli, bits of crispy bacon, herbs over a base of softened butter, plus a drizzle of honey for the sweetness Newt offers Leta during their school years. Toasted almonds are scattered evenly over the board to add another savoury layer. The board is served with bite-sized pieces of thinly sliced raisin bread toast points or crackers at your discretion, presented on a single tea tray.

FOR THE TOASTED ALMONDS

- 50g flaked almonds
- 1 tablespoon extra-virgin olive oil
- ¼ teaspoon salt
- ¼ teaspoon freshly ground black pepper

FOR THE BUTTER BOARD

- 4 rashers back bacon
- 225g butter, softened
- 1 tablespoon honey
- 70g broccoli florets, steamed and dried
- 1 tablespoon raisins
- 4 tablespoons chiffonade radicchio

FOR THE PRESENTATION

- Raisin bread or crackers

TO MAKE THE TOASTED ALMONDS

Preheat the oven to 180°C/160°C fan/Gas Mark 4. Line a baking sheet with baking paper.

In a small bowl, toss the almonds in the oil, salt and pepper. Arrange the almonds on the prepared baking sheet. Make sure the almonds do not overlap so that they can all colour. Bake for 20 minutes, stirring after 10 minutes. Remove from the oven and set aside to cool.

TO MAKE THE BUTTER BOARD

Cook the bacon rashers in a frying pan over a medium heat until crispy, 10–15 minutes. Drain on kitchen paper and set aside to cool. Dice into small pieces.

Use a round-bladed knife to spread the butter evenly across a board or serving platter. Drizzle the honey on top. Arrange the broccoli, bacon, raddichio and raisins evenly across the butter and honey. Scatter the toasted almonds evenly across the board.

Serve with toasted raisin bread or crackers.

Store the butter board in the refrigerator in an airtight container for 1–2 days, but it's best if eaten immediately. Store the bread at room temperature in an airtight container for 2–3 days.

YIELD: 12 SERVINGS
(2 MINI SANDWICHES EACH)

'GOOD GRAVY!' MINI MEAT LOAF TEA SANDWICHES

The 1920s contributed heaps of slang to the American language: 'Know your onions' (know what's up), 'juice joint' (a speakeasy), and 'sounds like berries to me!' (that's good!). Another was 'good gravy!' a way of expressing surprise or annoyance without using profanity, commonly used in New York City.

When Queenie Goldstein tries to leave MACUSA with Newt, Jacob and Tina hidden in Newt's case, she runs into her boss, Abernathy, who wonders why she's leaving so early. Queenie fakes being sick, but he continues his questioning – what's in the case? Brilliantly, she replies, 'Ladies' things.' This upsets Abernathy, but Queenie makes him jittery anyway, unnerving him even more, so he replies with the expression 'good gravy!' when she offers to let him take a look.

Inspired by this amusing scene, there's no better way to enjoy a bite-sized meat loaf sandwich than with a ketchup-based 'good gravy'.

FOR THE MEAT LOAF

30g butter

900g minced beef

80g red onion, diced

2 medium eggs

2 garlic cloves, very finely chopped

2 tablespoons finely chopped fresh parsley

100g dried breadcrumbs

80ml full-fat milk

1 teaspoon pink Himalayan sea salt

½ teaspoon freshly ground pepper

½ teaspoon mustard powder

½ teaspoon ground paprika

24 mini sandwich rolls

FOR THE 'GOOD GRAVY!'

1kg tomato ketchup

2 tablespoons cider vinegar

1 teaspoon paprika

1 garlic clove, very finely chopped

½ teaspoon freshly ground multicoloured pepper

¼ teaspoon pink Himalayan sea salt

Note ✦ The secret for the best meat loaf is to mix the ingredients well. And, like with any classic meat loaf, this is even better the next day or even 2 days after making it.

TO MAKE THE MEAT LOAF

Preheat the oven to 190°C/170°C fan/Gas Mark 5. Using 15g of butter, grease a 23 x 13cm loaf tin.

In a large bowl, combine the remaining 15g of butter, minced beef, onion, eggs, garlic, parsley, breadcrumbs, milk, salt, pepper, mustard and paprika. Using your hands, mix the ingredients together well, for 2–3 minutes.

Press the meat loaf mixture into the loaf tin, and bake until the edges become browned all around and pull away from the sides of the pan, 40–45 minutes.

Remove from the oven and set aside for a few minutes. When the meat loaf is no longer too hot to touch, slice it into 2.5cm-thick pieces.

TO MAKE THE 'GOOD GRAVY!'

Combine the ketchup, vinegar, paprika, garlic, pepper and salt in a mixing bowl, and stir until well combined.

To make a sandwich, place a piece of meat loaf and a tablespoon of the 'Good Gravy!' between two of the mini sandwich rolls.

Store the meat loaf in the refrigerator in an airtight container for 3–4 days. Store the bread at room temperature in an airtight container for 3–4 days.

'OH! GOOD GRAVY, NO!'

– Abernathy

Fantastic Beasts and Where to Find Them

'WILL YOU STOP EATING? YOUR BEST FRIEND IS MISSING!'

'TURN AROUND, YOU LUNATIC.'

– Hermione Granger and Ron Weasley

GF✻ ✦ YIELD: 12 SERVINGS

RON WEASLEY'S TEATIME RASPBERRY JELLY TREATS

When Harry Potter doesn't initially show up in the Great Hall after everyone else has departed the Hogwarts Express in *Harry Potter and the Half-Blood Prince*, Hermione takes out her concern by smacking Ron as he mindlessly shovels spoonfuls of a red jelly dish into his mouth.

Actress Emma Watson (Hermione) always thought that Hermione and Ron would end up together. 'I always thought there was a tension between them,' says Watson, 'and the reason they argue so much, and find each other so annoying, is they were so hyperaware of each other because they fancied each other.' Watson approved of the relationship, though. 'They're so wrong for each other, but so right.'

Harry finally turns up, and so, inspired by this sequence, this dish is a raspberry-flavoured layered jelly salad made in a mould. Layers include a basil-cream cheese spread and a soft pretzel base (or you can use bagels) that Ron surely wouldn't be able to stop eating.

FOR THE JELLY

15g butter, for greasing

150g strawberry or raspberry-flavoured jelly

425ml boiling water

425ml cold water

275g strawberries or raspberries

FOR THE PRETZEL MIXTURE

100g large soft pretzels or plain bagels, chopped

115g butter, softened

40g granulated sugar

NOTE ✦ For a gluten-free teatime treat, make this without the pretzel base.

TO MAKE THE JELLY

Use the butter to grease the holes of a 12-hole muffin tin.

Separate the jelly cubes and place them in a heatproof bowl. Add the boiling water and stir until dissolved, then stir in 425ml of cold water and the berries until combined. Pour the mixture into the holes in the prepared muffin tin, allowing at least a 1cm gap on top for the basil-cream cheese spread and the pretzel mixture. Chill in the refrigerator for at least 4 hours or until set.

TO MAKE THE PRETZEL MIXTURE

Blend the pretzels (or bagels), butter and sugar in a food processor until the pretzels are coarse and the mixture forms a dough-like consistency, about 5 pulses. Place the pretzel mixture in a small bowl and set aside until time to assemble. Clean the food processor to prepare it for making the basil-cream cheese layer.

CONTINUED ON PAGE 106

CONTINUED FROM PAGE 105

FOR THE BASIL CREAM CHEESE SPREAD

350g cream cheese, softened

200g granulated sugar

225g whipped cream

1 handful fresh basil

TO MAKE THE BASIL CREAM CHEESE SPREAD

Pulse the cream cheese, sugar and whipped cream in the food processor until well combined, about 3 pulses.

When the jelly is completely set, spread a thin layer of the cream cheese mixture on top of each jelly, followed by a layer of the pretzel mixture.

Use 2 large mixing spoons to delicately pull each of the moulded jellys out of the cavities of the muffin tin. If a jelly does not easily pull away from the muffin tin, dip the base of the tin in a sink filled with hot water for 2 seconds.

Garnish with the fresh basil, and serve each individual jelly on a plate, pretzel side down.

Store in the refrigerator in an airtight container for 2–3 days.

HAGRID'S BUTTERNUT SQUASH MINI TARTLETS WITH CRISPY BACON AND SAGE

V* ✦ YIELD: 6 SERVINGS

When Harry, Ron and Hermione visit Hagrid's hut in *Harry Potter and the Prisoner of Azkaban*, his garden is filled with gorgeous, bright orange pumpkins, which are one of many types of squash. And Hagrid may be growing other squashes there, such as butternut squash, with its, yes, buttery and nutty taste, used in this dish.

Hagrid's hut and its pumpkin patch were filmed in Scotland for *Prisoner of Azkaban*. Production designer Stuart Craig found the gorgeous backdrop and ample space to be gratifying – until filming began and it rained constantly! However, he did appreciate the different, 'serious energy' the rain clouds and shadows brought to the look of the sequence. Not surprisingly, it was one of the last times the crew shot extensively on location.

These rectangular-shaped puff pastry tartlets are topped with thin pieces of butternut squash tossed in a honey glaze, drops of cream cheese, fresh sage and bits of crispy fried bacon to create a dish Hagrid would surely be proud to serve visitors to his hut.

- ½ butternut squash, peeled and cut into quarters (thin tart slice-shaped pieces)
- 2 tablespoons extra-virgin olive oil
- 1 tablespoon honey
- 1 pinch pink Himalayan sea salt
- 1 dash freshly ground multicolour pepper
- 2 tablespoons chopped fresh sage
- ½ packet ready-prepared frozen puff pastry
- 1 egg

Preheat the oven to 180°C/160°C fan/Gas Mark 4. Line a baking sheet with baking paper.

In a large mixing bowl, combine the squash, oil, honey, salt, pepper and sage. Toss for 1 minute, then set aside to marinate.

Cut the pastry into 5 x 10cm rectangles, and arrange the pieces on the prepared baking sheet. The pastry will yield 6–8 rectangles. Whisk the egg in a small bowl and use a pastry brush to paint the egg on each of the pastry pieces.

CONTINUED ON PAGE 109

'COME IN. I'VE JUST MADE A POT OF TEA.'

– Rubeus Hagrid

Harry Potter and the Chamber of Secrets

CONTINUED FROM PAGE 107

- 2 tablespoons cream cheese
- 2 rashers bacon, fried until crispy and chopped

Note: For a vegetarian option, make these without bacon.

Place 3 tablespoons of the squash and sage mixture on top of each of the pieces of pastry. Scatter tiny bits of cream cheese and bacon on the top of each pastry piece. Drizzle the remaining oil from the squash and sage mixture over each tartlet.

Leave the tartlet open, with no pastry on top.

Bake until each pastry piece is baked all the way through and brown on the tops and edges, 40–45 minutes.

Remove the tartlets from the oven and serve warm.

Store in the refrigerator in an airtight container for 3–4 days.

YIELD: 75 MEATBALLS
OR 25 SERVINGS

AUNT PETUNIA'S TEATIME HAM BITES

In *Harry Potter and the Chamber of Secrets*, the Dursleys host the affluent Masons for dinner, and Vernon is adamant the evening goes well. 'He doesn't want anything strange happening that the neighbours might see,' Richard Griffiths (Vernon) said. 'The Dursleys want to be ordinary, average and normal, and Harry Potter prevents the possibility of all this, which is terrifying to them.' Petunia has done her best to prepare a dinner that will please their guests, but Vernon's worst fears are realised when the dinner ends in disaster.

These ham bites would be a perfect dish to serve no matter the occasion but are a great item for a high tea. The warm meatballs are drizzled with a tangy glaze made from fruits such as pineapples or peaches and from Scotch whisky. Serve them with a small piece of pineapple, a maraschino cherry and a sprig of fresh pineapple mint. Arrange these on a tea tray, but separate them from other foods so that the light juice on each meatball does not mix with other items.

FOR THE MEATBALLS

450g freshly minced ham

450g freshly minced beef

75g crushed crackers

3 eggs

250ml full-fat milk

1 red pepper, deseeded and diced

2 tablespoons mustard powder

3 garlic cloves, very finely chopped

2 tablespoons fresh marjoram leaves

½ teaspoon pink Himalayan sea salt

½ teaspoon freshly ground pepper

FOR THE GLAZE

150g apricot, pineapple, or elderberry jam

1 tablespoon Scotch whisky

1 tablespoon chicken or vegetable stock

FOR THE CONDIMENTS

325g pineapple jam

325 apricot jam

275g tomato ketchup

'NOT NOW, POPKIN, FOR WHEN THE MASONS ARRIVE.'

– Petunia Dursley

Harry Potter and the Chamber of Secrets

TO MAKE THE MEATBALLS

Preheat the oven to 180°C/160°C fan/Gas Mark 4. Line a baking sheet with baking paper.

In the bowl of a stand mixer or in a large mixing bowl using your hands, combine the ham, beef, crackers, eggs, milk, red pepper, mustard, garlic, 1 tablespoon of the marjoram leaves, the salt and pepper. Mix until combined well, but take care not to over-mix so that the meatballs do not become overly dense.

Use a small ice-cream scoop to create 2.5cm balls. Using your hands, roll each ball until it is smooth all around.

Arrange the meatballs on the prepared baking sheet 2.5cm apart. Bake until the edges become browned, about 1 hour.

TO MAKE THE GLAZE

In a small saucepan over a medium-high heat, combine the jam, Scotch and stock, and bring to the boil. Reduce the heat to medium and simmer, stirring occasionally, until blended well, about 15 minutes.

Remove the meatballs from the oven, drizzle with glaze and scatter over the remaining 1 tablespoon marjoram leaves. Serve on a platter with bamboo cocktail sticks alongside three small clear glass bowls filled with pineapple jam, apricot jam and ketchup.

Store in the refrigerator in an airtight container for 3–4 days.

GF* ✦ YIELD: 18 MINI HOT DOGS

TINA GOLDSTEIN'S BITE-SIZED HOT DOGS WITH HONEY MUSTARD SAUCE

In *Fantastic Beasts and Where to Find Them*, Newt Scamander meets the former Auror Tina Goldstein on the steps of Steen National Bank while she watches Mary Lou Barebone, head of the New Salem Philanthropic Society, campaign to expose and wipe out wizarding kind in a fiery speech. Tina watches, eating a hot dog, which leaves a smear of mustard on her lip.

As one passion of Tina's sister, Queenie, is cooking, graphic artists Miraphora Mina and Eduardo Lima filled the Goldstein flat with cookbooks, including one on how to cook like a No-Maj, called *Franks and Human Beans*. The book just happens to have a recipe for apple strudel in it. In addition to that recipe and others in the book, Mina and Lima provided the labels for the flour and sugar products used when Queenie bakes.

These savoury mini hot dogs, aka cocktail sausages, are served in little buns with a honey mustard sauce. Napkins are a must, so as not to end up with mustard on your lip like Tina!

FOR THE MINI HOT DOGS

450g bread dough, thawed if frozen

800g cocktail sausages

Note ✦ For a gluten-free savoury teatime treat, offer mini hot dogs without the bun, presented on a bamboo cocktail stick.

FOR THE HONEY MUSTARD

2 tablespoons mustard powder

1 tablespoon mustard seeds

3 tablespoons honey

¼ teaspoon cider vinegar

½ teaspoon turmeric

¼ teaspoon pink Himalayan sea salt

¼ teaspoon freshly ground black pepper

> 'ER. YOU'VE GOT SOMETHING ON YOUR -'
>
> – Newt Scamander to Tina Goldstein
>
> *Fantastic Beasts and Where to Find Them*

TO MAKE THE MINI HOT DOGS

Preheat the oven to 180°C/160°C fan/ Gas Mark 4. Line two baking sheets with baking paper.

Cut the bread dough into 5cm pieces and roll them into oval shapes. The dough will yield 18–20 mini hot dog buns.

Place 18 of the bread dough ovals on one of the prepared baking sheets and bake until golden brown around the edges and lightly browned on top, 50–60 minutes.

Place the cocktail sausages on the second baking sheet, and bake until dark brown all around, about 40 minutes.

Remove the mini breads and the cocktail sausages from the oven, and set aside to cool for 2–3 minutes.

Use a serrated knife to cut the mini breads horizontally on one side. Do not cut all the way through.

TO MAKE THE HONEY MUSTARD

Combine the mustard powder, mustard seeds, honey, vinegar, turmeric, salt and pepper in a large mixing bowl, and use a spoon to mix together well.

Place a mini hot dog in each bun, and top with a line of honey mustard.

Store the hot dogs in the refrigerator in an airtight container for 2–3 days. Store the mustard in the refrigerator in an airtight container for 2–3 weeks. Store the bread at room temperature in an airtight container for 3–4 days.

YIELD: 8 SERVINGS

RON WEASLEY'S SAVOURY ESCARGOT-STUFFED MUSHROOMS

When Ron Weasley crashes into the Whomping Willow at Hogwarts in *Harry Potter and the Chamber of Secrets*, he breaks his wand. He fastens it with sticky tape, but the wand is still wonky. Later, defending Hermione after Draco insults her, Ron casts 'Eat slugs!' but the spell backfires and Ron ends up expectorating a trio of gastropods.

That scene was one of Rupert Grint's (Ron) favourites. 'I had to put these giant slugs in my mouth and then spit them out with all this lovely goo,' says Grint. The slime of the three plastic slugs used, which were named Monty, Vincent and Ethel, were flavoured with chocolate, lemon, orange and peppermint.

Escargots are a French delicacy that taste a bit like mussels. Arrange these escargot-stuffed mushrooms in classic French escargot plates, with a bamboo cocktail stick in each so that guests can eat them in one bite.

- 2 tablespoons extra-virgin olive oil
- 200g canned escargot, rinsed, drained and finely chopped
- 115g crab, fresh or canned, drained
- 2 tablespoons diced red onion
- 1 tablespoon diced fresh red pepper
- 1 tablespoon dried breadcrumbs
- ¼ teaspoon mustard powder
- 60g fresh parsley leaves (no stalks), chopped
- 125ml pinot grigio or other dry white wine
- 1 fresh lemon
- ½ teaspoon freshly ground multicolour pepper
- ¼ teaspoon pink Himalayan sea salt
- 15g butter, at room temperature
- 24 medium and large button mushrooms
- 2 tablespoons grated Parmesan cheese
- 1 lemon, cut into 5mm-thick wedges

Preheat the oven to 180°C/160°C fan/Gas Mark 4.

In a frying pan over a medium heat, heat the oil. Add the escargot, crab, onion, red pepper, breadcrumbs, mustard, 40g of the parsley, the wine, juice from ½ the lemon, pepper and salt. Use a spoon to combine the ingredients together well. Cook, stirring occasionally, for about 30 minutes.

With the butter, grease a 23cm flan tin or 20cm square baking dish.

Brush off the mushrooms to remove any soil, and pull the stalk out from the centre of each mushroom. Arrange the mushrooms in the prepared baking dish, top side down, so that the openings are facing up.

Use a spoon to stuff the escargot mixture into each mushroom cap. Stuff as much of the mixture into each mushroom as the mushroom will hold. Capacity will vary with size of each mushroom.

Scatter the mushrooms with the Parmesan cheese, and bake until the stuffing and mushrooms are baked together and the mushrooms become much darker, 30–40 minutes.

Remove from the oven and serve hot, scattered with the remaining 20g of fresh parsley and the lemon wedges.

Store in the refrigerator in an airtight container for 1–2 days, but they're best if eaten immediately when fresh and warm.

'EAT SLUGS!'

– Ron Weasley

Harry Potter and the Chamber of Secrets

V ✦ YIELD: 4 SERVINGS

KOWALSKI BAKERY'S BUTTERY TEATIME WITCH HATS WITH MAGICAL HERBAL BROOMSTICKS

When Jacob Kowalski opens his bakery after the memory of his time in the wizarding world is Obliviated, in *Fantastic Beasts and Where to Find Them*, it's stocked with breads, cakes and something much more unusual: pastry versions of beasts the Muggle world has never seen before. 'There's this subliminal sort of memory that's coming out in what he's baking,' says prop modeler Pierre Bohanna. And so, pastry versions of Demiguises, Nifflers, Erumpents and Occamys are sold alongside the rolls and paczki. 'Obviously they're not *real* breads,' Bohanna adds about the synthetic creatures cast in moulds, 'but they're beautiful artworks.'

Inspired by this idea, serve these witch hat-shaped breads on small plates with a dollop of heart-shaped butter, using the herbal 'broomstick' to spread the butter. The broomsticks, inspired by Harry's state-of-the-art Firebolt broomstick, are a mix of thyme, dill and tarragon on a 'handle' made of rosemary. The herbs add fresh flavours to both the butter and bread.

FOR THE WITCH HATS

450g bread dough, thawed if frozen

125g plain flour

4 black olives

FOR THE HERBAL BROOMSTICKS

2 x 10cm sprigs fresh rosemary

4 x 5cm sprigs fresh tarragon

4 x 5cm sprigs fresh dill

4 x 5cm sprigs fresh oregano

16 x 13cm sprigs fresh chives

TO MAKE THE WITCH HATS

Preheat the oven to 180°C/160°C fan/Gas Mark 4.

Place a piece of baking paper in the base of 2 aluminium baking tins with 5cm-deep sides.

Scatter some flour on the work surface for the dough.

Using a knife, cut the bread dough into thirds to create rectangles. Pull one end into a curved point. Make a small 5mm slit in the other end and pull the two sides of the cut into a hat brim shape as desired. Use a sharp knife to cut some slits into the hat body for texture. Brush with butter and bake for 15–30 minutes.

Remove the breads from the oven, leaving them in their tins to cool on the work surface.

CONTINUED ON PAGE 119

CONTINUED FROM PAGE 117

FOR THE GARLIC BUTTER SAUCE

225g butter

1 garlic clove, very finely chopped

1 tablespoon fresh tarragon leaves

1 tablespoon chopped fresh dill

1 tablespoon chopped fresh oregano

1 tablespoon chopped fresh chives

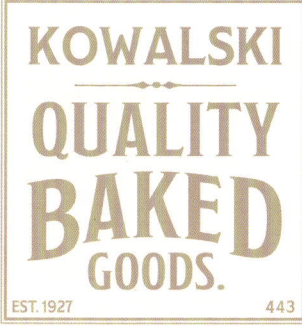

When the breads have cooled enough to touch, divide the bread among 4 plates, and place a herbal broomstick alongside the bread on the plate.

TO MAKE THE HERBAL BROOMSTICKS

Strip the leaves from the sprigs of rosemary, leaving the top ⅓ in place. Arrange one sprig each of the tarragon, dill and oregano around the top part of the rosemary.

Place the chives in a damp sheet of kitchen paper and microwave for 20 seconds. Divide the chives into 4 equal-sized parts, and tie them around the herbs to secure them at the top of the rosemary sprigs. Serve a broomstick on each plate to use as a brush to apply the butter to the bread.

Store the breads at room temperature in an airtight container for 3–4 days. Store the butter in the refrigerator in an airtight container for 6–7 days. Store the herbs in the refrigerator in an airtight container for 2–3 days.

TO MAKE THE GARLIC BUTTER SAUCE

Just before serving, melt the butter in a glass bowl in the microwave. Stir in the garlic, tarragon, dill, oregano and chives and mix well. Serve alongside the breads.

> 'WHERE DO YOU GET YOUR IDEAS FROM, MR KOWALSKI?'
>
> 'I DON'T KNOW, I DON'T KNOW – THEY JUST COME!'
>
> – Female Customer to Jacob Kowalski
>
> *Fantastic Beasts and Where to Find Them*

MOLLY WEASLEY'S BANGERS AND ROASTED TOMATO QUICHE BITES

YIELD: 24 SERVINGS

Actress Julie Walters calls her character 'a mother who happens to be a witch. She's a sweet person, and the most real of them in so many ways,' she adds. Walters maintains that no matter what is happening around her, 'she's a force for good, a force for all the good stuff in the world: love, family and what's good about humanity.'

These small teatime quiches, which can be eaten in two bites, are inspired by what Mrs Weasley might make for her family and guests at lunchtime, but with a full English twist. Although quiche is often considered a French dish, the name is actually German for 'cake'. This popular item is extremely adaptable, with a custardy base of milk, cream and eggs. Then it's all about the add-ins! Sausages and roasted tomatoes aren't just for an English full breakfast, but can be served with quiche for a mash-up of breakfast and lunch.

FOR THE ROASTED TOMATOES

- 5 large vine-ripened tomatoes
- 3 tablespoons extra-virgin olive oil
- 2 garlic cloves, very finely chopped
- 1 teaspoon coarse salt
- ¼ teaspoon freshly ground black pepper

NOTE ✦ Almost any shredded soft cheese will work well; however, Gruyère cheese provides the most authentic flavour of a classic French quiche.

For a gluten-free option, these can also be made without the pastry.

TO MAKE THE ROASTED TOMATOES

Preheat the oven to 180°C/160°C fan/Gas Mark 4.

Chop the tomatoes into quarters. Place the tomatoes on a baking sheet, and drizzle with the olive oil. Scatter over the garlic, salt and pepper. Roast for 30–40 minutes, stirring after the first 20 minutes.

Remove the tomatoes from the oven, and set on a plate lined with kitchen paper on the work surface to cool. Place a piece of kitchen paper on top of the tomatoes, and gently press to absorb some of the oil.

CONTINUED ON PAGE 123

'COME ON, HARRY. TIME FOR A SPOT OF BREAKFAST. HERE WE ARE, HARRY. TUCK IN. THAT'S IT. THERE WE GO.'

– Molly Weasley

Harry Potter and the Chamber of Secrets

CONTINUED FROM PAGE 121

FOR THE QUICHE

- 2 sheets shortcrust pastry, at room temperature
- 450g sausages
- 8 medium eggs
- 500ml milk
- 250ml double cream
- 120g Gruyère cheese, grated
- 100g Parmesan cheese, grated
- 2 teaspoons mustard powder
- 80g red onion, diced
- 40g fresh basil, chopped
- ¼ teaspoon freshly ground black pepper
- 15g butter, for greasing

✦ BEHIND THE MAGIC ✦

'Although she has all these magicky things,' says Julie Walters about Molly Weasley, 'there's something very down-to-earth about her.'

TO MAKE THE QUICHE

Roll out the dough and use a 5cm round biscuit cutter to cut the dough into 25 round pieces.

In a large frying pan over a medium heat, brown the sausages, 20–30 minutes. Turn the sausages over as the brown on each side until browned all around.

In a large mixing bowl, use a fork to break the egg yolks and gently beat the eggs, 1–2 minutes. Add the milk, cream, 60g of the Gruyére cheese, the Parmesan cheese, mustard, onion, 35g of the basil and the pepper, and use a large spoon to mix together. Combine thoroughly. Cut the browned sausages into 5mm round pieces and add to the mixing bowl. Add the roasted tomatoes. Mix well.

Use the butter to grease the rounds of two 12-hole cupcake tins. Place one of the pastry rounds in each of the cupcake holes, using your fingers to shape the pastry so that it covers the inside of each hole. Pat around the edges at the top to smooth out the pastry all around. Use a fork to pierce holes in the base of each round of pastry.

Place 250ml of the mixture into each round in the cupcake holes, ensuring that each type of ingredient is in every round. Scatter the remaining 60g Gruyére cheese on top.

Bake until the quiches become the consistency of custard and the edges are dark brown, 40–45 minutes.

Scatter with remaining 5g of basil before serving.

Store in the refrigerator in an airtight container for 3–4 days.

CHAPTER THREE

TEATIME SWEETS, SNACKS AND TAKE-HOME GIFTS

GF, V, V+* ✦ YIELD:
6 FROGS

FROGGY FANCIES

Chocolate Frogs are an extremely popular wizarding treat. The five-sided box created to house the jumping confection was designed by graphics department artist Ruth Winick, based upon input by production designer Stuart Craig. 'Stuart drew the shape of a pentagon and said I should think "classical",' says Winick. She looked at Gothic architecture as a source for the packaging. On the top of the Chocolate Frog box are images that evoke the trefoil windows that are the Gothic style of Hogwarts castle. The graphics department was also responsible for adding ingredients, slogans and establishing dates of the Honeydukes sweets.

The melted chocolate here is sweetened by blackberry flavouring for a warming lift. Thankfully, these treats inspired by the Chocolate Frogs sold by Honeydukes in *Harry Potter and the Philosopher's Stone* won't jump out a window before you can eat them!

- 350g chocolate chips
- 2 tablespoons rice crisp cereal
- 1 teaspoon blackberry extract

SPECIALIST TOOLS

- 1 sheet frog-shaped plastic moulds
- Cooking spray

Note ✦ For a vegan option, use dairy-free chocolate chips.

> 'THESE AREN'T REAL FROGS. ARE THEY?'
>
> 'IT'S JUST A SPELL.'
>
> – Harry Potter to Ron Weasley
>
> *Harry Potter and the Philosopher's Stone*

In a heatproof bowl set over a saucepan of simmering water, or in a microwave-safe bowl in the microwave, melt the chocolate. If using the microwave, microwave for 1 minute, stirring after 30 seconds. Add the rice crisp cereal and the blackberry extract, and stir well to combine thoroughly. The mixture will become stiff, like the consistency of a biscuit dough.

Spray cooking spray inside the frog moulds. Wipe away any excess with a soft cloth.

Using your fingers, place the chocolate mixture into each of the frog moulds. Spread the chocolate throughout each of the moulds, ensuring that the chocolate is the same thickness all over. Press in around the edges so that all of the chocolate is inside the mould. Push down on top of each mould that is filled with chocolate to flatten and smooth out the tops.

CONTINUED ON PAGE 128

CONTINUED FROM PAGE 127

Place the moulds in the refrigerator until the chocolate is firm enough to remove it from the moulds without breaking, about 4 hours.

Once set, carefully pull the chocolate from the moulds. Arrange the frogs on a serving platter. Create a platter with a mix of the Divination Dream Bar Tea Treats (page 20), Feverless Fudge Tea Bites (page 129), Dumbledore's Elderberry Tea Pastilles (page 143), Dementors Mini Chocolate Teatime Treats (page 136), Disenchantment Tea Jellies (page 133) or Chocolate Flying Keys (page 139).

Store at room temperature in an airtight container for 5–6 days.

✦ BEHIND THE MAGIC ✦

The label for Chocolate Frogs includes information that 70 per cent of a Chocolate Frog contains the finest *croakoa* – a mash-up of 'croak' and 'cacao,' aka 'cocoa bean', the seed from which chocolate is made.

GF, V ✦ YIELD: 24 BITE-SIZED PIECES

FEVERLESS FUDGE TEA BITES

In their fifth year at Hogwarts, Fred and George Weasley began a business selling the Skiving Snackbox, which contains sweets that allow a student to feign illness to leave class, with the antidote on the other side of the sweet. But students were not the only targets. One of the box's bestsellers – Fever Fudge – was used on Argus Filch when he was caught spying on the newly created Dumbledore's Army in *Harry Potter and the Order of the Phoenix*.

When Fred and George leave Hogwarts to pursue careers as entrepreneurs, they establish a joke shop on Diagon Alley, in *Harry Potter and the Half-Blood Prince*. Weasleys' Wizard Wheezes sells fireworks, jokes and sweets, including Fever Fudge. Prop makers used about 300 litres of silicone in a variety of revolting colours to make the sweets they sell.

These minty, chocolaty, marshmallowy *feverless* fudge bites won't cause the same reaction of Fever Fudge – just a smile and sigh at its sweet, bright flavour.

- 600g granulated sugar
- 175g butter
- 160ml evaporated milk
- 115g mint chocolate chips
- 225g milk chocolate chips
- 200g marshmallow cream
- 55g mini marshmallows
- 1 teaspoon peppermint extract
- 1 tablespoon fresh chocolate mint leaves

Place baking paper in a 23 x 30cm baking tin, ensuring that the paper goes up the sides of the tin. For thicker pieces of fudge, use a 20cm square baking dish.

In a medium saucepan over a high heat, combine the sugar, butter and evaporated milk. Bring to a rolling boil. Continue to boil for 4 minutes, stirring the mixture constantly. Remove from the heat. Use a spoon to quickly mix in the mint chocolate and milk chocolate chips. When the chocolates are thoroughly mixed in, add the marshmallow cream and combine well. Add the mini marshmallows and peppermint extract, and stir well to combine, ensuring the peppermint flavour is incorporated well.

Pour the fudge mixture into the prepared baking tin. Set this aside to cool and firm up, about 4 hours. Cut the fudge into tiny pieces. Garnish with fresh mint leaves, chiffonade or whole, and serve on a small plate.

Store at room temperature in an airtight container for 2–3 weeks.

> 'STEP UP, STEP UP! WE'VE GOT FAINTING FANCIES, NOSEBLEED NOUGAT, AND JUST IN TIME FOR SCHOOL, PUKING PASTILLES!'
>
> – Fred and George Weasley
>
> *Harry Potter and the Half-Blood Prince*

'YOUR GRANDFATHER KEPT PIGEONS? MINE BRED OWLS. I USED TO LOVE FEEDING 'EM.'

– Queenie Goldstein to Jacob Kowalski

Fantastic Beasts and Where to Find Them

GRANDFATHER GOLDSTEIN'S TEATIME OWL FOOD

GF, V ✦ YIELD: 18–20 SERVINGS IN SMALL SNACK CUPS; 4–6 SERVINGS IN PRESERVING JARS

After Queenie Goldstein rescues Newt, Tina and Jacob from MACUSA headquarters, where the Director of Magical Security had imprisoned them, the quartet finds themselves regrouping on a New York rooftop that features a pigeon coop. Jacob's recollection from his past brings up a fond memory in Queenie.

Queenie and Tina Goldstein were orphaned at an early age, their parents having passed from dragon pox. 'Tina and Queenie are each other's family,' says Alison Sudol (Queenie). Though they may be opposites in personality and style, 'It's very easy for Queenie to just love Tina. You don't need to prove how much you love somebody if you love them enough, and that's how I feel with Tina and Queenie.'

This roasted fruit and nut snack inspired by the Goldstein sisters' grandfather includes ingredients that appeal to humans as well as owls. Serve this as a finger snack, or package them in preserving jars to give to your guests to take home.

- 125g walnuts
- 150g almonds
- 125g cashew nuts
- 80g dried strawberries
- 125g dried blueberries
- 65g dried mango, cut into 1cm pieces
- 80g dried apricots, cut into 1cm pieces
- 350g honey
- 15g butter, melted
- 1 tablespoon fresh thyme leaves
- ¼ teaspoon salt flakes
- ¼ teaspoon freshly ground multicoloured pepper

Preheat the oven to 180°C/160°C fan/Gas Mark 4. Line a baking sheet with baking paper.

In a large bowl, combine the walnuts, almonds, cashews, strawberries, blueberries, mango, apricots, honey, butter, thyme, salt and pepper, and stir until combined well.

Spread the mixture out on the prepared baking sheet. Roast until the strawberries start to become slightly dark around the edges, 20–25 minutes.

Remove from the oven and set aside to cool to room temperature.

Store at room temperature in an airtight container for 2–3 weeks.

'SURGITO!'

– Newt Scamander

Fantastic Beasts: The Crimes of Grindelwald

GF, V ✦ YIELD: 24
HEART-SHAPED JELLIES

DISENCHANTMENT TEA JELLIES

As Newt works with the beasts in his house in London in *Fantastic Beasts: The Crimes of Grindelwald*, he finds that Queenie Goldstein and Jacob Kowalski have let themselves in for a visit. But over dinner, Newt realises that something is off with Jacob – he shakes salt on his hand instead of his food, and he toasts his engagement to Queenie by splashing a glass of champagne into his face!

'Jacob is being unnaturally jolly,' says Dan Fogler. 'I'm a little bit too happy. It turns out Queenie has put me under her spell.' A very *specific* spell. When Newt performs the *Surgito* spell on Jacob to remove Queenie's love enchantment, a bright red heart appears above Jacob's head.

These heart-shaped jellies inspired by *Surgito* are made with raspberry tea. They can be set out in a bonbon dish, arranged among other teatime sweets on a tea tray, or packaged in a container for guests to take home.

135g cherry, raspberry or strawberry jelly

285ml boiling water

115g unflavoured powdered gelatine

300g cherry, raspberry or strawberry jam

SPECIALIST TOOLS

2 sweets moulds with 12 x 5cm heart shapes

Cooking spray

Separate the jelly into cubes, place in a saucepan and pour in the boiling water. Stir until dissolved. Add the powdered gelatine and jam and place over a low heat until thickened, about 4 minutes, stirring constantly.

Spray a heart-shaped sweets mould with cooking spray. Wipe away any excess with a damp, soft cloth.

Use a small spoon to carefully fill each of the hearts.

Place in the refrigerator until the hearts set, about 1 hour.

Use a plastic knife to remove the hearts by putting the knife into the base of each heart and carefully and lightly pushing the knife around between the jelly and the mould, and pulling the jelly out of each mould.

Serve the hearts on a serving tray or place a few in small clear plastic sweetie bags, tied with ribbon, for guests to take home with them.

Store in the refrigerator in an airtight container for 5–6 days.

'FROZEN ASHWINDER EGG!'

– Newt Scamander's offer to Gnarlak at The Blind Pig

Fantastic Beasts and Where to Find Them

GF, V ✦ YIELD: 12 SERVINGS

PICKLED 'ASHWINDER' EGGS

As Newt pursues his missing beasts in *Fantastic Beasts and Where to Find Them,* Tina suggests he see Gnarlak, the goblin owner of The Blind Pig speakeasy, who trades in magical creatures and might have seen one. Newt realises that he'll have to make it worth Gnarlak's while to get information, and so offers Galleons, a Lunascope and finally a frozen Ashwinder egg, used most often in love potions.

'A guy in Gnarlak's position just knows how to make deals with every stratum,' says Ron Perlman, who plays the seedy goblin, 'be it the highest stations in government or the lowest form of criminality and nefariousness.'

Pickled eggs are a common sight in drinking establishments; these hard-boiled eggs are pickled in white wine vinegar with bay leaves and juniper berries. Serve these in a shallow bowl or give each guest a few in a preserving jar to take home with twine or ribbon tied around the lid of the jar.

200g granulated sugar

250ml white wine vinegar

2 bay leaves

10 dried juniper berries

5 cloves

12 eggs, hard-boiled

1 large beetroot, cut into 2.5cm pieces

✦ BEHIND THE MAGIC ✦

Gnarlak passes on the Ashwinder egg after spotting Newt's Bowtruckle, Pickett. (Bowtruckles can pick locks.)

In a medium saucepan over a medium-high heat, combine the sugar, vinegar, 250ml of water, the bay leaves, juniper berries and cloves. Bring to the boil, then reduce the heat to medium.

Place the eggs and beetroot in a large bowl or in preserving jars. Pour the liquid mixture over the eggs and beetroot. Cover the eggs, and let them pickle in the mixture for at least 1 day; keep them refrigerated.

Slice each egg into quarters, and serve the pieces of egg on a plate mixed with the Salade Niçoise Teatime Boat Bites (page 80), Durmstrang Institute Shopska Salad Tea Party Boats (page 77), Ron Weasley's Finger Sandwich Bites (page 83), Aunt Petunia's Teatime Ham Bites (page 110) or Tina Goldstein's Bite-Sized Hot Dogs with Honey Mustard Sauce (page 112). Or, give each guest 2 or 3 eggs in a preserving jar to take home with them.

Store in the refrigerator in an airtight container for 1–2 months.

V, V+*
YIELD: 12 SERVINGS

DEMENTORS MINI CHOCOLATE TEATIME TREATS

According to Professor Remus Lupin, Dementors feed on every good feeling and every happy memory a person has. They greatly affect Harry Potter upon their first appearance in *Harry Potter and the Prisoner of Azkaban*, as he had few happy childhood memories until he came to Hogwarts.

Prisoner of Azkaban director Alfonso Cuarón wanted the Dementors to have a completely different quality from the other creatures seen on screen, and one way to achieve this was with their very slow motions. He instructed the digital artists that Dementors are not in any hurry and should move like royalty, describing them as 'a force you cannot stop. And I think we created truly scary creatures,' he adds.

Crunchy and coconuty, these Dementors have a chocolaty *goodness* that will only generate happy memories.

- 75g desiccated coconut
- 680g chocolate chips
- 30g butter, softened
- 275g dried Chinese noodles
- 1 tablespoon coarse salt flakes

NOTE ✦ For a vegan option, use dairy-free chocolate chips and butter.

Preheat the oven to 180°C/160°C fan/Gas Mark 4. Line a baking sheet with baking paper.

Place the coconut on the prepared baking sheet. Bake until lightly browned, about 8 minutes, stirring after about 3 minutes. Remove from the oven and set aside.

Place the chocolate chips and butter in a medium microwave-safe mixing bowl. Melt the chocolate chips in the microwave, stirring about every 20 seconds, just until the chocolate is completely melted.

Add the dried noodles and the toasted coconut to the melted chocolate. Stir to combine, making sure that every noodle is generously covered in chocolate.

✦ BEHIND THE MAGIC ✦

One way to defend against these cheerless, gloomy creatures is to cast *Expecto Patronum* – a spell that creates a positive force the Dementor feeds upon instead of the caster.

Place a 30cm piece of greaseproof paper on the work surface. Use an ice-cream scoop to form balls with the chocolate coated noodles. Place the balls on the greaseproof paper. Scatter coarse salt flakes over the top of each ball. Let the balls dry for about 1 hour or longer. When dry, arrange the balls on a serving platter. Create a platter with a mix of the Divination Dream Bar Tea Treats (page 20), Feverless Fudge Tea Bites (page 129), Dumbledore's Elderberry Tea Pastilles (page 143), Froggy Fancies (page 127), Disenchantment Tea Jellies (page 133) or Chocolate Flying Keys (page 139).

Store at room temperature in an airtight container for 2–3 weeks.

> **'DEMENTOR! DEMENTOR!'**
>
> – Draco Malfoy trying to upset Harry Potter
>
> *Harry Potter and the Prisoner of Azkaban*

> 'CURIOUS. I'VE NEVER SEEN BIRDS LIKE THESE.'
>
> 'THEY'RE NOT BIRDS – THEY'RE KEYS. AND I'LL BET ONE OF THEM FITS THAT DOOR.'
>
> – Hermione Granger and Harry Potter
>
> *Harry Potter and the Philosopher's Stone*

GF, V, V+* ✦ YIELD: 7 KEYS

CHOCOLATE FLYING KEYS

In *Harry Potter and the Philosopher's Stone*, Harry, Hermione and Ron are challenged three times after they drop through a trapdoor in their search of the film's titular artefact. Hermione helps when they become entangled in Devil's Snare. Ron plays the 'best played game of chess that Hogwarts has seen these many years,' to quote Headmaster Dumbledore. And Harry uses his incredible talents on a broomstick to catch a winged key that will allow them access to the final challenge.

The digitally created keys were designed to be scary and wild – if they were beautiful, they would lose their threat to the young wizards. Their movement was also an important factor, and it was decided the keys would move in concert like a flock of birds, swirling and shooting around Harry as he flies around the room to catch the right key.

These one- or two-bite chocolate keys have a sweet raspberry flavour that helps counteract the bitterness of melted chocolate, giving them a fruity lightness and raising them to a new level. They'll fly off the plate!

350g chocolate chips

1 tablespoon raspberry extract

14 edible wings

SPECIALIST TOOLS

1 plastic key-shaped candy mould

Cooking spray

NOTE ✦ For a vegan option, use dairy-free chocolate chips.

In a heatproof bowl set over a saucepan of simmering water, or in a microwave-safe bowl in the microwave, melt the chocolate. If using the microwave, microwave for 1 minute, stirring after 30 seconds. Add the raspberry extract and stir well. The mixture will become stiff like the consistency of a biscuit dough.

Spray cooking spray inside the key-shaped moulds. Wipe away excess with a soft cloth.

Using your fingers, place the chocolate mixture in the key moulds. Spread the chocolate throughout each of the moulds, ensuring the chocolate is the same thickness all over. Press in around the edges so that all of the chocolate is inside the mould. Push down on top of each mould that is filled with chocolate to flatten and smooth out the tops.

CONTINUED ON PAGE 140

CONTINUED FROM PAGE 140

Place the moulds in the refrigerator until the chocolate is firm enough to remove it from the moulds without breaking, about 4 hours.

Once set, carefully pull the chocolate from the moulds.

Press a hot round-bladed knife into the sides of each key at the top, and press an edible wing in on each side.

Tie a string ribbon around the handle of each key and hang the keys in a doorway, fireplace mantel or window frame.

Store at room temperature in an airtight container for 2–3 weeks.

GF, V, V+
YIELD: 10 LOLLIPOPS

HONEYDUKES TAKE-HOME LOLLIPOPS

When Harry Potter finally makes his way to Honeydukes sweet shop in Hogsmeade (via the Marauder's Map as he cannot get his permission slip signed), he wears his Invisibility Cloak. Making his way through the shop, he 'lifts' a shiny red lollipop from Neville Longbottom just as he's about to take a lick!

As seen in *Harry Potter and the Prisoner of Azkaban*, Honeydukes is packed with tall glass jars filled with sweets set in front of mint-green walls with candy-floss-coloured shelf accents. In addition to the sweets, two displays feature eye-popping automatons. A top-hatted skeleton dispenses Eyeball Bonanza jawbreakers that are collected through his toothy mouth. The other is a bearded man tangling with house-elves who pull his hair. He dispenses strings of liquorice from his beard.

Neville was enjoying a 'blood pop' before Harry grabbed it upon his exit. These bright red lollipops are raspberry flavoured. Place them on a tea tray by the door where guests can pick one up to take home.

Cooking spray
300g granulated sugar
160g golden syrup
½ teaspoon cream of tartar
2 teaspoons raspberry extract
10 drops red food colouring

SPECIALIST TOOLS

Sugar thermometer
1 sheet of lollipop moulds with 10 moulds on the sheet
10 x 5cm-long lollipop sticks (these come with many lollipop moulds)

Spray the lollipop moulds with cooking spray. Set the mould on a baking sheet.

In a large saucepan over a medium heat, combine the sugar, 175ml of water, the golden syrup and cream of tartar. Bring the mixture to the boil and continue to cook until the temperature reaches 150°C/130°C fan/Gas Mark 2 on a sugar thermometer. Remove from the heat, and stir in the raspberry extract and the food colouring until the colouring is completely blended into the mixture and there are no streaks.

Use a large spoon to put 1 teaspoon of the mixture into each of the cavities of the lollipop candy mould. Insert a stick into each of the moulds, ensuring that ⅔ of the stick extends outside of the lollipop. Let the lollipop mould rest on the work surface until the lollipops are completely hardened, about 45 minutes. Pull each lollipop out of its mould, and wrap a 5cm square piece of clingfilm around the lollipop. Twist the ends of the clingfilm around the lollipop stick to close the plastic around the lollipop.

Store at room temperature in an airtight container for 3–5 weeks.

GF, V
YIELD: 24 SWEETS

DUMBLEDORE'S ELDERBERRY TEA PASTILLES

Albus Dumbledore has a well-known affection for sweets. After all, the password to enter the winding staircase to his office is 'Sherbet Lemon.' And he keeps a bowl of bite-happy Liquorice Snaps on his desk. He would probably love these sweet teatime treats – and one reason could be in the name. After all, he wields the Elder Wand!

The props department was tasked with creating all the sweets, pastries, and other confections that appear at sweet shops such as Honeydukes. Thousands of silicone candies were moulded for Weasleys' Wizard Wheezes. And for the wedding of Bill Weasley and Fleur Delacour in *Harry Potter and the Deathly Hallows – Part 1*, four thousand small cakes, petits fours and other bite-sized confectioneries were crafted (along with a four-tiered cake).

These entrancing sweeties are made with elderberry jam in the form of a pastille – a small treat meant to melt in your mouth.

300g elderberry jam

1 tablespoon honey

2 tablespoons unflavoured powdered gelatine

100g granulated sugar

15g butter

125g icing sugar

Line a small baking dish with baking paper, being careful to line the sides of the dish.

In a medium saucepan over a high heat, combine the jam, honey, gelatine, granulated sugar and butter, and bring to the boil. Boil for 4 minutes, stirring constantly. The mixture will become thick.

Pour the mixture into the prepared baking dish. Allow it to sit until the mixture is formed and becomes thick enough that a knife is needed to cut it, at least 4 hours.

Use a knife to cut the sweets, in the dish, into 2.5cm rectangles or squares.

Place the icing sugar in a medium bowl. Remove the sweets from the dish where they formed and add the 2.5cm pieces to the icing sugar. Toss them in the sugar until they are coated all around. Let the sweets sit in an airtight container overnight in the refrigerator. Arrange the sweets on a small plate to serve them.

Store in the refrigerator in an airtight container for 1–2 weeks. Remove the sweets from the refrigerator 1 hour before serving so they can be served at room temperature.

'OH, HARRY, DO FEEL FREE TO INDULGE IN A LITTLE LIQUORICE SNAP IN MY ABSENCE. BUT I HAVE TO WARN YOU, THEY'RE A WEE BIT SHARP.'

– Albus Dumbledore
Harry Potter and the Goblet of Fire

CHAPTER FOUR

TEATIME TIPPLES, HOT DRINKS AND MAGICAL MIXES

HOGWARTS HOUSE TEAS

GF, V ✦ YIELD: 1 SERVING (PER TEA)

House pride at Hogwarts means displaying your house colours, whether it's on your robes or on banners cheering on your house Quidditch team. There's a very special item in Hogwarts' Great Hall that showcases the house colours: the house points hourglasses set behind the professors' high table. House points are gained or lost by students, culminating in the awarding of the House Cup at the end of the school year. The hourglasses were fully functional, and careful attention was paid to place the beads at the top compartment at the beginning of each school year, as no points had been won yet.

This selection of teas represents each of the Hogwarts houses in colour and flavour. The rosy red of geraniums evokes Gryffindor red. A ginger tea with honey suggests the yellow of Hufflepuff; butterfly pea flower conjures up the Ravenclaw blue. And a lemony green mint tea represents Slytherin house.

These house-colourful teas would perfectly accompany the Hogwarts Houses Four-Layer Rainbow Petits Fours (page 65)!

FOR THE HONEYED GINGER HUFFLEPUFF TEA

- 1 tablespoon chopped fresh ginger
- ¼ teaspoon clover honey
- 5 drops yellow food colouring

BUTTERFLY PEA FLOWER RAVENCLAW TEA

- 1 tablespoon crushed dried butterfly pea flowers
- ¼ teaspoon lemon juice
- ¼ teaspoon honey

TO MAKE THE HONEYED GINGER HUFFLEPUFF TEA

Fill a teacup with hot water. Place the ginger in a tea infuser and add it to the hot water. Infuse for 2 minutes. Add the honey and yellow food colouring and stir 3 revolutions with a spoon.

TO MAKE THE BUTTERFLY PEA FLOWER RAVENCLAW TEA

Fill a teacup with hot water. Place the dried butterfly pea flowers in a tea infuser and place the infuser in the hot water. Infuse the tea for 1 minute. Add the lemon and honey, and stir to combine.

CONTINUED ON PAGE 149

> 'FIVE POINTS WILL BE AWARDED TO EACH OF YOU. FOR SHEER DUMB LUCK!'
>
> – Minerva McGonagall to Harry Potter and Ron Weasley
>
> *Harry Potter and the Philosopher's Stone*

CONTINUED FROM PAGE 147

FOR THE LEMONY MINT SLYTHERIN TEA

- 1 tablespoon chopped fresh mint leaves
- ½ thin slice fresh lemon
- 1 drop green food colouring

FOR THE STRAWBERRY-SCENTED GERANIUM GRYFFINDOR TEA

- 1 tablespoon crushed dried scented geranium leaves
- 1 drop red food colouring
- 1 fresh scented geranium leaf
- 3 dried strawberry slices

TO MAKE THE LEMONY MINT SLYTHERIN TEA

Fill a teacup with hot water. Place the mint in a tea infuser and add the infuser to the hot water. Infuse for 2 minutes. Add the fresh lemon and the green food colouring, and stir.

TO MAKE THE STRAWBERRY-SCENTED GERANIUM GRYFFINDOR TEA

Fill a teacup with hot water. Place the dried geranium leaves in a tea infuser. Place the tea infuser in the hot water. Infuse for 1 minute.

Remove the tea infuser, and add the red food colouring. Stir the colour into the tea until well blended.

Garnish with 1 fresh scented geranium leaf and the dried strawberry slices.

✦ **BEHIND THE MAGIC** ✦

Tens of thousands of glass beads were used in the house points hourglasses, which caused a shortage of beads in Britain!

GF, V, V+
YIELD: 1 SERVING

GINGER WITCH WHISKY SOUR

Whisky sours were popular cocktails in New York City in the 1930s, and this gingery version, inspired by a unique, unseen character in the wizarding world, will be popular among your royal tea guests, with a perfect blend of sweet and sour.

To fill the columns of *The Daily Prophet*, graphic designers Miraphora Mina and Eduardo Lima wrote titles about Quidditch matches, author appearances and contest winners. There has also been one reoccurring character called the 'Ginger Witch', who has had a career as a criminal from the 1920s to at least the 1990s. Her first appearance is in *Harry Potter and the Prisoner of Azkaban*, but her hooliganism dates back to the days of *Fantastic Beasts and Where to Find Them*.

FOR THE GINGER SIMPLE SYRUP

- 100g granulated sugar
- 1 tablespoon chopped fresh ginger

FOR THE COCKTAIL

- 50ml Scotch whisky
- 25ml fresh lemon juice

FOR THE GARNISH

- ½ thin slice fresh lemon
- 1 maraschino cherry

TO MAKE THE GINGER SIMPLE SYRUP

In a small saucepan over a high heat, bring the sugar, 125m of water and the ginger to the boil. Stir constantly, and boil until the sugar is completely dissolved. Reduce the heat to medium and allow the mixture to simmer for 30 minutes. Remove from the heat and set aside to cool to room temperature. Strain the ginger from the liquid by pouring the liquid through a handheld fine-mesh sieve into a large bowl.

TO MAKE THE COCKTAIL

Fill a coupe glass ⅔ full with ice. Add the whisky to the glass with ¼ of the ginger simple syrup and the lemon juice, then stir well.

Garnish with the lemon slice and cherry on a bamboo cocktail stick.

Use the extra ginger simple syrup for flavouring teas, cocktails and desserts. Store in the refrigerator in an airtight container for 2–3 days.

✦ **BEHIND THE MAGIC** ✦

Throughout her notorious career, the Ginger Witch has been prosecuted for wig theft, implicated in a product recall of Bertie Bott's Every Flavour Beans, and was arrested at a Muggle football match.

'MYSTERIOUS GINGER WITCH UNDER INVESTIGATION'

– *The Daily Prophet*, November 1926

Fantastic Beasts and Where to Find Them

GF, V ✦ YIELD: 1 SERVING

TEDDY THE NIFFLER'S MILK TREAT

Teddy the Niffler, who stole our hearts in *Fantastic Beasts and Where to Find Them*, becomes a bit of a scamp in *Fantastic Beasts: The Crimes of Grindelwald*, though his thieving ways prove vital to helping Dumbledore defeat Grindelwald. Teddy was able to swipe the vial that contains their blood oath to never fight each other.

Inspirations for the Niffler's amusing look and spirited character came from moles, platypuses and echidnas. Video references of these animals using their paws were studied. 'We also found great footage of a honey badger ransacking somebody's house,' says visual effects supervisor Christian Manz. 'It was just an insatiable desire for food, going through fridges and cupboards. Those real-world animalistic traits went into the Niffler, which is why I think he's so successful.'

This malted milk treat with fresh whipped cream would be a worthy reward for Teddy's actions in stealing the vial. Chocolate sprinkles on top pay tribute to the Niffler's spiky black fur.

FOR THE MALTED MILK DRINK

- 2 tablespoons chocolate syrup
- 1 tablespoon chocolate sprinkles (see note)
- 250ml full-fat milk
- 55g malted milk powder

FOR THE WHIPPED CREAM TOPPING

- 125ml double cream
- 1 teaspoon granulated sugar
- ½ teaspoon lemon juice

NOTE ✦ Use 5mm-long dark brown chocolate sprinkles that look like Niffler's spiky fur.

TO MAKE THE MALTED MILK DRINK

Place the chocolate syrup on a plate, then dip the rim of a clear glass into the chocolate. Swirl the rim around in a circular motion to ensure that the entire rim is coated with the chocolate syrup.

Place the chocolate sprinkles on a separate large plate. Place the rim of the glass into the sprinkles, and roll the rim around to ensure that sprinkles coat the entire rim of the glass.

In a mixing glass, use a barspoon to mix the milk with the malted milk powder. Stir briskly until the powder dissolves and the milk and powder are combined well, about 2 minutes.

TO MAKE THE WHIPPED CREAM TOPPING

In the bowl of a stand mixer or a large mixing bowl with a hand mixer, beat the double cream, sugar and lemon juice together on low until well combined and starting to thicken so it won't splatter, about 3 minutes. Increase the speed to high and beat the cream until thickened enough to form soft peaks, 12–15 minutes.

Pour the drink into the clear glass and top with 2 tablespoons of the whipped cream topping.

Store in the refrigerator in an airtight container for 1–2 days.

GF, V
YIELD: 16 SERVINGS

TREVOR'S TOAD POND PUNCH

Neville Longbottom brings a toad with him to his first year at Hogwarts and loses him – twice – in *Harry Potter and the Philosopher's Stone*. Four toads shared the role of Trevor, Neville's often-misplaced companion. The real name of the toad most frequently on screen was, coincidentally, Harry. However, this Harry did not enjoy being held and would try to jump out of Matthew Lewis's (Neville's) hands into his face or on to other actors.

In spite of this, Lewis enjoyed the humour Trevor brought to the story and would raise a glass to him of this fizzy lemon-lime soda with an apple-flavoured Kool-Aid mix (available in specialist food suppliers, or use food-grade citric acid and a few drops of green food colouring as a substitute). Serve this frothy treat in a punch bowl as your substitute 'toad pond', or in individual clear, stemmed wine or coupe glasses.

- 2 litres lemon-lime soda, chilled
- 115g powdered green apple–flavoured drink mix
- 1.5 litres ice
- 1.5 litres lemon or lime gelato or sorbet

SPECIALIST TOOLS

Clear glass punch bowl and ladle

In a jug or a punch bowl, combine the soda and powdered drink mix. Mix together until the powder is completely dissolved, 3–5 minutes.

Add the ice. Add spoonfuls of the gelato or sorbet all around the punch bowl and in the centre.

Serve these with Divination Dream Bar Tea Treats (page 20) that have been cut into the shapes of lily pads using a flower-shaped or a lily pad–shaped biscuit cutter.

Store in the refrigerator in an airtight container for 1–2 days.

ALBUS DUMBLEDORE'S APPLE BUTTER AND BRANDY HOT TODDY

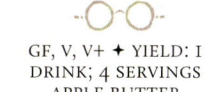

GF, V, V+ ✦ YIELD: 1 DRINK; 4 SERVINGS APPLE BUTTER

In *Harry Potter and the Prisoner of Azkaban*, Harry and Hermione use her Time-Turner to save Hagrid's Hippogriff, Buckbeak, by leading him away and hiding him after the creature had been sentenced for execution. Once it's learnt that Buckbeak is nowhere to be found, the executioner is dismissed, and Albus Dumbledore gestures for Minister for Magic Cornelius Fudge to join him in Hagrid's hut for a cup of tea, or better yet, a brandy.

'We talked about having the Hippogriff sitting down in the pumpkin patch,' says creature effects supervisor Nick Dudman. 'And I said, "We can do that." It would be attached to a chain the kids will tug on. I said we could do that, too. And then they said Buckbeak would get up and walk away with them. And I said, "Ah, no. I don't think we can do that!"'

On days like the cold, rainy ones over which this sequence was shot, this apple-buttery hot drink spiced with cinnamon and mint would have been greatly appreciated by the cast and crew.

FOR THE APPLE BUTTER

- 2 large Pink Lady or Jazz apples, peeled and cut into 2.5cm pieces
- 2 tablespoons soft brown sugar
- Juice of 1 lemon
- 1 teaspoon ground cinnamon
- ¼ teaspoon grated nutmeg

FOR THE DRINK

- 50ml brandy
- 50ml hot water
- ½ teaspoon fresh lemon juice

FOR THE GARNISH

- 2 thin slices fresh Pink Lady or Jazz apple
- 2 large mint leaves
- 1 cinnamon stick

TO MAKE THE APPLE BUTTER

In a small saucepan over a high heat, combine the apples, 250ml of water, the brown sugar, lemon juice, cinnamon and nutmeg. Bring the mixture to the boil, stirring constantly, until thickened, about 4 minutes. Reduce the heat to medium, and simmer for 40 minutes.

Store in the refrigerator in an airtight container for 4–5 days.

TO MAKE THE DRINK

Pour the brandy in a clear glass mug; add the hot water and the lemon juice. Stir, then add 1 tablespoon of the apple butter. Stir rapidly.

Garnish with 2 very thin slices of fresh apple and 2 large mint leaves on a cocktail stick; add the cinnamon stick as a stirrer.

> 'WELL SEARCH THE SKIES IF YOU MUST, MINISTER. MEANWHILE, I'D LIKE A NICE CUP OF TEA OR A LARGE BRANDY.'
>
> – Albus Dumbledore
>
> *Harry Potter and the Prisoner of Azkaban*

GF, V, V+ ✦ YIELD: 1 SERVING

PROFESSOR TRELAWNEY'S DIVINATION TEA

Professor Sybill Trelawney's first lesson for her Divination class in *Harry Potter and the Prisoner of Azkaban* is the art of reading tea leaves, where each student reads the cup of the person sitting opposite them. Ron reads Harry's and interprets the shapes of the tea leaves as being Harry will suffer but be happy about it. When Trelawney looks into Harry's cup, she sees the Grim, a giant spectral dog that is an omen of death.

This drink features lime (linden) leaves, which not only make for a great-tasting tea, but they also have been used throughout history for divination purposes. Dreaming of a lime tree itself portends good news in the future! Once you've drunk the tea, you might want to try your own hand at tessomancy with the leftover leaves.

20 large dried lime tree leaves

One ½-inch lemon slice

Use a pestle and mortar to crush the lime tree leaves into a fine, sandy consistency, about 5 minutes. Place the crushed tree leaves into a tea infuser. Fill a teacup ¾ full with hot water. Add the infuser and stir. Add the lemon.

After the tea has been consumed, study the pattern of the remaining tea sediment.

✦ BEHIND THE MAGIC ✦

'I think she has a genuine gift,' says actress Emma Thompson of Trelawney. 'But like all those [who do this], she has to make it stretch. She has to make it bigger than it actually is.' Trelawney's predictions have a tendency towards gloom and doom, which Thompson believes helps to 'ratchet things up.'

'THIS TERM WE SHALL BE FOCUSING ON TESSOMANCY, WHICH IS THE ART OF READING TEA LEAVES. SO PLEASE, TAKE THE CUP OF THE PERSON SITTING OPPOSITE YOU.'

– Sybill Trelawney

Harry Potter and the Prisoner of Azkaban

V, V+* ✦ YIELD: 1 SERVING

GOLDSTEIN SISTERS' COINTREAU HOT CHOCOLATE

While staying at the Goldstein sisters' flat in *Fantastic Beasts and Where to Find Them*, Tina offers Newt and Jacob hot cocoa as a soothing bedtime treat. Jacob tries to get Newt to join him, but the Magizoologist seems to be asleep. However, once Tina leaves, Newt jumps out of bed and descends inside his case, beckoning for an amazed Jacob to follow him. The No-Maj is enchanted at the magical creatures inside.

Building upon Tina's chocolate beverage, for this drink, each guest's teacup has a shot of Cointreau, an orange-flavoured liqueur, and a chocolate ball filled with mini marshmallows and edible gold glitter. After the host pours hot milk over the chocolate ball, guests stir rapidly until the chocolate ball melts into the steamy milk, releasing the marshmallows and edible gold glitter. Royal tea guests will surely be as spellbound as Jacob was with Tina's cocoa as they enjoy the hot chocolate 'magic' of this delightful drink.

45g chocolate chips

1 teaspoon butter

5 mini marshmallows

¼ teaspoon edible gold lustre dust and glitter

250ml full-fat milk

1 tablespoon Cointreau

1 teaspoon orange zest

SPECIALIST TOOLS

1 sheet of plastic sweet moulds to make 5cm hollow chocolate balls

NOTE ✦ For a vegan option, make this with hot water in place of hot milk and use carob chips in place of milk chocolate chips.

In a large microwave-safe bowl in the microwave or in a heatproof bowl set over a saucepan of simmering water, melt the chocolate and butter just until the chips are all completely melted and the butter and chocolate are blended together thoroughly. If melting the chocolate in the microwave, heat the chocolate on medium for 1 minute, stir and heat for 1 minute more.

Using a pastry brush, coat the inside of each of the halves of the ball mould evenly with the chocolate. Pull the chocolate up along the sides to the top edge of the ball mould all around. Repeat this multiple times all around, until the inside of each mould is covered about 5mm thick with chocolate. Use a clean round-bladed knife to go around the edge of the moulds, evening out the chocolate around the edges.

Place the mould in the refrigerator until the chocolate hardens enough to stand on its own once the mould is removed, 10–15 minutes.

When the chocolate has set, remove the mould from the refrigerator, and pull the chocolate ball away from the mould. Using a pastry brush, go around the edge of the top and bottom halves of the mould with hot water so that the chocolate softens just enough so that both the top and bottom halves of the mould will stick when they are brought together.

Place 5 mini marshmallows and ¼ teaspoon edible gold dust in the centre of one of the halves of the chocolate ball. Bring the halves of the ball together so that the edges line up, and lightly press until the halves are secured together, about 3 minutes. Place the ball in the refrigerator to harden together well, about 3 minutes.

In a small saucepan over a high heat, bring the milk to the boil. Reduce the heat to a medium-low and simmer the milk until it is time to pour it.

Pour 1 tablespoon of Cointreau in a mug, then place a chocolate ball in the mug.

Put the hot milk in a teapot, and pour the hot milk into the mug.

Garnish with orange zest.

Stir rapidly to help release the glitter, marshmallow and chocolate from the ball as it melts under the heat of the milk. Stir continually until milk and chocolate are combined well.

✦ BEHIND THE MAGIC ✦

The base of Newt's case and the floor below it were removed for his descent. Then a ladder was placed inside for Eddie Redmayne to disappear down. Dan Fogler's character, Jacob, was a tighter fit trying to get into the case. Jacob gets himself inside with a few 'jumps' – a bit of digital movie magic.

'I THOUGHT YOU MIGHT LIKE A HOT DRINK?'

– Tina Goldstein

Fantastic Beasts and Where to Find Them

THE NEW YORK GHOST WAKE-UP CALL DRAMBUIE BREW

GF, V, V+*
YIELD: 2 SERVINGS

The New York Ghost, the local wizarding newspaper in *Fantastic Beasts and Where to Find Them*, advertises a robust caffeine-type drink called 'Wakey-Up Brew'. The wizarding world's java pick-me-up may be rivalled in getting your get-up-and-go going by this very strong, anise-flavoured coffee drink, flavoured with Drambuie, a special Scotch whisky. It's a dynamic addition to any royal tea.

The graphics department was tasked with creating the many newspapers published in the wizarding world since *The Daily Prophet* in the Harry Potter films. They also came up with ideas for the advertisements and article titles that peppered the papers. In order to give the paper that worn newsprint look, the pages were dipped into a special coffee blend, then laid out on the floor in the hallways to dry. Due to this, every newspaper seen in the wizarding world films has a slight coffee smell to it.

FOR THE WHIPPED CREAM

250ml double cream
1 teaspoon granulated sugar
Juice of ¼ fresh lemon

FOR THE DRAMBUIE COFFEE

250ml ice
125ml Drambuie
500ml brewed coffee, cooled to room temperature

FOR THE GARNISH

2 sprigs fresh mint
1 pinch edible gold lustre dust and sparkles

NOTE ✦ To make a vegan option, replace the whipped cream with a nondairy cream.

TO MAKE THE WHIPPED CREAM

In the bowl of a stand mixer or a large mixing bowl with a hand mixer, beat the whipping cream, granulated sugar and lemon juice together on low until well combined and starting to thicken so it won't splatter, about 3 minutes. Increase the speed to high and beat the cream until thickened enough to form soft peaks, 12–15 minutes.

TO MAKE THE DRAMBUIE COFFEE

Fill each of 2 clear glass coffee mugs with 125ml of the ice. Pour 50ml of the Drambuie over the ice in each glass, followed by 250ml of the coffee. Top each glass with the whipped cream.

Garnish with a sprig of fresh mint and edible gold lustre dust and sparkles.

> 'POSSIBLY MORE POTENT THAN NO-MAJ COFFEE!'
>
> – Advertisement in *The New York Ghost* for Wakey-Up Brew
>
> *Fantastic Beasts and Where to Find Them*

> 'YOU'RE GOING TO BE DOING SOME LINES FOR ME TODAY, MR POTTER. NO, NOT WITH YOUR QUILL. YOU'RE GOING TO BE USING A RATHER SPECIAL ONE OF MINE.'
>
> – Dolores Umbridge
>
> *Harry Potter and the Order of the Phoenix*

GF, V, V+ ✦ YIELD: 1 SERVING

PROFESSOR UMBRIDGE'S EARL GREY TEA AND RASPBERRY CHAMPAGNE COCKTAIL

Before Dolores Umbridge supervises Harry at his detention in her office, in *Harry Potter and the Order of the Phoenix*, she makes herself a cup of tea, stirring in at least three teaspoons of pink sugar. However, she does not seem to stir her tea correctly according to teatime 'rules' – she stirs it in a circle instead of backwards and forwards – but she does hold her cup correctly, with a firm grasp on the handle, no little finger askew.

Regarding Harry's detention, '[Umbridge] thinks that's perfectly fair,' says Imelda Staunton. However, the actress found it alarming that Umbridge uses punishment as a way of teaching, and stated that she felt terrible after filming the scene.

This royal tea tipple is inspired by the tea service and the pink colours in scenes featuring Professor Umbridge. For a nonalcoholic option, you can make these with lemon-lime soda in place of champagne.

1 ice cube

250ml champagne or sparkling wine, chilled

1 tablespoon brewed, infused Earl Grey tea, at room temperature

½ teaspoon granulated sugar

4 fresh raspberries, divided

Place the ice cube into a champagne or wineglass.

In a mixing glass, combine the champagne and tea, and stir.

In a separate glass or in a bowl, use the back of a large spoon to muddle the sugar and 3 raspberries, and add this to the mixing glass.

Stir the ingredients together until well blended, about 15 revolutions with a barspoon.

Pour the mixture over the ice. Garnish with the remaining raspberry set on a bamboo cocktail stick; rest it across the rim of the glass.

'I'VE BEEN STUDYING HIM. AND I'M PRETTY SURE HIS VENOM COULD BE QUITE USEFUL IF PROPERLY DILUTED. JUST TO REMOVE BAD MEMORIES, YOU KNOW.'

– Newt Scamander

Fantastic Beasts and Where to Find Them

GF, V, V+ ✦ YIELD: 1 SERVING

SWOOPING EVIL BLUEBERRY AND MINT AVIATION COCKTAIL

Newt Scamander's been travelling the world, rescuing, rehabilitating and learning as much as he can about magical creatures, including one the locals call the Swooping Evil – 'not the friendliest of names,' Newt says. Through his knowledge, Newt knows he can use the venom from the Swooping Evil to Obliviate the memory of 1927 New York City's residents after the destruction caused by the Obscurial Credence Barebone. The venom is distributed by a Thunderbird, another creature Newt rescued, who creates a rainstorm that disperses the contents of a blue-coloured vial.

The creature designers referenced both butterflies and bats for the Swooping Evil, whose underside is coloured a rich cobalt blue. Its head resembles that of a rodent, with sharp, saber-shaped teeth. However 'evil' it looks, it is only helpful to Newt and his friends.

This Swooping Evil cocktail, perfect for a royal tea, is a refreshing, minty spin on the classic aviation cocktail. A hint of blueberry balances out the violet flavour.

- 3 plump blueberries, divided
- 1 large sprig fresh mint
- 250ml ice
- 50ml gin
- 1½ teaspoons crème de violette
- 1 tablespoon fresh lemon juice
- 1 pinch lemon zest
- 1 pinch edible gold lustre dust and tiny stars

Muddle 1 blueberry and 3 mint leaves by grinding them together using a pestle and mortar. In place of a pestle and mortar, mash the ingredients in a small bowl, using a spoon.

In a cocktail shaker, combine the ice, gin, crème de violette, lemon juice and the muddled blueberry and mint. Shake for 20 revolutions.

Strain into a coupe glass. Place the remaining 2 blueberries and a large sprig of fresh mint on a bamboo cocktail stick, and place across the rim of the glass as a garnish. Scatter the top with lemon zest and the edible gold lustre dust.

✦ MUGGLE MAGIC ✦

The aviation cocktail was invented in New York City in the early 20th century. Its name comes from the sky-blue colour that results from the use of crème de violette, which is a nod to a time when air travel was still a new and glamorous form of transport.

GF, V, V+ ✦ YIELD: 1 SERVING

PROFESSOR SNAPE'S BLUEBERRY-SAGE SPRITZER

Professor Severus Snape is a very 'buttoned-up' type of wizard, very reserved and not inclined to reveal his thoughts. He's also 'buttoned up' literally – buttons run up to his neck, up his long sleeves and even on his trousers over his boots.

This magical mix was inspired by Snape's blue robes, which photographed black on film, and the idea that maybe, in a moment of relaxation, he would set his mind to creating a refreshing, energising beverage instead of a potion. For a royal tea option, substitute sparkling wine for the sparkling water.

Buttons were one of the stipulations Alan Rickman requested when his costume was designed. Rickman knew his costume was an important indication of the very focused life that Snape led. 'You know he lives a solitary existence; you're not quite sure what the details of that are. He doesn't have much of a social life, and clearly, he's only got one set of clothes!' he said.

- 70g fresh blueberries
- 1 teaspoon coarse sugar crystals
- 1 teaspoon freshly chopped sage leaves, plus 3 whole fresh leaves
- 250ml sparkling water

NOTE ✦ This is a refreshing nonalcoholic drink, but you can replace the sparkling water with sparkling wine for a more intoxicating option.

Using a pestle and mortar, muddle together 35g of the blueberries, the sugar and the 1 teaspoon of freshly chopped sage leaves.

Fill a large clear glass half full with ice. Place the blueberry sage mixture and the remaining 35g of blueberries into the glass, followed by the sparkling water. Stir this together well. Add the 3 whole sage leaves as garnish.

'I CAN TEACH YOU HOW TO BEWITCH THE MIND AND ENSNARE THE SENSES.'

– Severus Snape to his first-years' Potions class

Harry Potter and the Philosopher's Stone

DIETARY CONSIDERATIONS

SWEET FINGER TREATS AND SUGARY NIBBLES

Hagrid's Pumpkin Teatime Madeleines ✦ V

Jacob Kowalski's Mini Teatime Paczki ✦ V

Nicolas Flamel's French Fancies ✦ V

Hogwarts High Table Roasted Apple Scone Bites with Fresh Cream and Mint ✦ V

Divination Dream Bar Tea Treats ✦ V

Aunt Petunia's Teatime Windtorte Pudding ✦ GF, V

Hungarian Horntail Mini Teatime Cakes ✦ V

Professor Umbridge's Load of Waffles ✦ V

Paris Pâtisserie Two-Bite Lavender Teatime Canelés ✦ V

Professor McGonagall's Transfigurational Sticky Toffee Pudding Bites ✦ V

Molly Weasley's Individual Teatime Rhubarb and Custard Trifles ✦ V

Professor Slughorn's One-Bite High Tea Profiteroles ✦ V

Kowalski Bakery's Occamy Egg Teatime Surprise ✦ GF, V

Honeydukes Lemon Drop Meringue Teatime Bites ✦ V

One-Bite Circus Animal Tea Biscuits ✦ V

Queenie's Mini Brandied Apple Strudels with Apple Mint Sauce ✦ GF, V

Professor Sprout's Bite-sized Greenhouse Mystery Cakes ✦ V

Place Cachée Orange-Scented Teatime Pastry Puffs ✦ V

Hogwarts Houses Four-Layer Rainbow Petits Fours ✦ V

Dolores Umbridge's I Will Make Scones

Teddy the Niffler's Two-Bite Gold Coin Sandwich Cakes ✦ V

Queenie Goldstein's Floating Teapot ✦ GF, V

SAVOURY TEATIME FINGER FOODS

Durmstrang Institute Shopska Salad Tea Party Boats ✦ GF, V

Mini Fried Raven Egg Tea Sandwiches ✦ GF

Salade Niçoise Teatime Boat Bites ✦ GF

Ron Weasley's Finger Sandwich Bites

Leaky Cauldron Split Pea Teatime Soup ✦ GF

Forbidden Forest Mini Mushroom Strudels ✦ V

Luna Lovegood's Honey-Roasted Radish Salad ✦ GF, V

Black Lake Cod Cakes with Poached Eggs and Brandy Cream Sauce ✦ GF

Deathly Hallows Pull-Apart Teatime Bread ✦ V

Great Hall Treacle and Pinot Noir–Roasted Turkey Drumsticks ✦ GF

Bowtruckle Island Butter Board ✦ GF

'Good Gravy!' Mini Meat Loaf Tea Sandwiches

Ron Weasley's Teatime Raspberry Jelly Treats ✦ GF

Hagrid's Butternut Squash Mini Tartlets with Crispy Bacon and Sage ✦ V

Aunt Petunia's Teatime Ham Bites

Tina Goldstein's Bite-Sized Hot Dogs with Honey Mustard Sauce ✦ GF

Ron Weasley's Savoury Escargot-Stuffed Mushrooms

Kowalski Bakery's Buttery Teatime Witch Hats with Magical Herbal Broomsticks ✦ V

Molly Weasley's Bangers and Roasted Tomato Quiche Bites

TEATIME CANDIES, SNACKS, AND TAKE-HOME GIFTS

Froggie Fancies ✦ GF, V, V+

Feverless Fudge Tea Bites ✦ GF, V

Grandfather Goldstein's Teatime Owl Food ✦ GF, V

Disenchantment Tea Jellies ✦ GF, V

Pickled 'Ashwinder' Eggs ✦ GF, V

Dementors Mini Chocolate Teatime Treats ✦ V, V+

Chocolate Flying Keys ✦ GF, V, V+

Honeydukes Take-Home Lollipops ✦ GF, V, V+

Dumbledore's Elderberry Tea Pastilles ✦ GF, V

TEATIME TIPPLES, HOT DRINKS, AND MAGICAL MIXES

Hogwarts House Teas ✦ GF, V

Ginger Witch Whisky Sour ✦ GF, V, V+

Teddy the Niffler's Milk Treat ✦ GF, V

Trevor's Toad Pond Punch ✦ GF, V

Albus Dumbledore's Apple Butter and Brandy Hot Toddy ✦ GF, V, V+

Professor Trelawney's Divination Tea ✦ GF, V, V+

Goldstein Sisters' Cointreau Hot Chocolate ✦ V, V+

The New York Ghost Wake-Up Call Drambuie Brew ✦ GF, V, V+

Professor Umbridge's Earl Grey Tea and Raspberry Champagne Cocktail ✦ GF, V, V+

Swooping Evil Blueberry and Mint Aviation Cocktail ✦ GF, V, V+

Professor Snape's Blueberry-Sage Spritzer ✦ GF, V, V+

FRY STATION SAFETY TIPS

If you're making something that requires deep-frying, here are some important tips to keep you safe:

✦ If you don't have a dedicated deep-fryer, use a large, high-sided saucepan or pot.

✦ Never have too much oil in the pan! You don't want hot oil spilling out as soon as you put the food in.

✦ Use only a suitable cooking oil, such as rapeseed, groundnut or vegetable oil.

✦ Always keep track of the oil temperature with a thermometer; 175–190°C should do the trick.

✦ Never put too much food in the pan at the same time!

✦ Never put wet food in the pan. It will splatter and can cause burns.

✦ Always have a lid nearby to cover the pan, in case it starts to spill over or catch fire. A properly rated fire extinguisher is also great to have to hand in case of emergencies.

✦ Never leave the pan unattended, and never allow children or pets near the pan.

✦ Never, ever put your face, your hand or any other body part in the hot oil.

METRIC CONVERSION CHART

KITCHEN MEASUREMENTS

MILLILITRES	UK FL OZ	SPOONS	US CUPS
15ml	½fl oz	3 tsp/1 tbsp	1/16 cup
30ml	1fl oz	2 tbsp	⅛ cup
60ml	2fl oz	4 tbsp	¼ cup
80ml	2¾fl oz	5½ tbsp	⅓ cup
120ml	4fl oz	8 tbsp	½ cup
160ml	5½fl oz	10⅔ tbsp	⅔ cup
180ml	6½fl oz	12 tbsp	¾ cup
240ml	8½fl oz	16 tbsp	1 cup

ML/LITRES	UK FL OZ	UK PINTS	US CUPS	US FL OZ
300ml	10.5fl oz	½ pint	1¼ cups	10fl oz
568ml	20fl oz	1 pint	2⅜ cups	19¼fl oz
1 litre	35fl oz	1¾ pints	4¼ cups	34fl oz
1.2 litres	42¼fl oz	2 pints	5 cups	40½fl oz
2 litres	70fl oz	3½ pints	8½ cups	67½fl oz

WEIGHT

GRAMS	OUNCES
15 g	½ oz
28–30 g	1 oz
55 g	2 oz
85 g	3 oz
115 g	4 oz
140 g	5 oz
175 g	6 oz
285 g	10 oz
400 g	14 oz
450 g	16 oz
900 g	32 oz

OVEN TEMPERATURES

CELSIUS	FAHRENHEIT
95°C	200°F
110°C	225°F
120°C	250°F
140°C	275°F
150°C	300°F
160°C	325°F
180°C	350°F
190°C	375°F
200°C	400°F
220°C	425°F
230°C	450°F

LENGTH

METRIC	IMPERIAL
2.5 cm	1 in
5 cm	2 in
10 cm	4 in
15 cm	6 in
20 cm	8 in
25 cm	10 in
30 cm	12 in

INDEX

Albus Dumbledore's Apple Butter and Brandy Hot Toddy, 157

almonds
  Bowtruckle Island Butter Board, 101
  Grandfather Goldstein's Teatime Owl Food, 131
  Place Cachée Orange-Scented Teatime Pastry Puffs, 62–63

apples
  Albus Dumbledore's Apple Butter and Brandy Hot Toddy, 157
  Hogwarts High Table Roasted Apple Scone Bites with Fresh Cream and Mint, 18–19
  Professor McGonagall's Transfigurational Sticky Toffee Pudding Bites, 37–39
  Queenie's Mini Brandied Apple Strudels with Apple Mint Sauce, 57–59

Aunt Petunia's Teatime Ham Bites, 110–111

Aunt Petunia's Teatime Windtorte Pudding, 23–25

bacon
  Bowtruckle Island Butter Board, 101
  Hagrid's Butternut Squash Mini Tartlets with Crispy Bacon and Sage, 107–109
  Ron Weasley's Finger Sandwiches, 83–84

beef
  Aunt Petunia's Teatime Ham Bites, 110–111
  'Good Gravy!' Mini Meat Loaf Tea Sandwiches, 102–103

biscuits
  Hagrid's Pumpkin Teatime Madeleines, 13
  One-Bite Circus Animal Tea Biscuits, 53–55

Black Lake Cod Cakes with Poached Eggs and Brandy Cream Sauce, 92–93

blueberries
  Grandfather Goldstein's Teatime Owl Food, 131
  Professor Snape's Blueberry-Sage Spritzer, 169
  Swooping Evil Blueberry and Mint Aviation Cocktail, 167
  Bowtruckle Island Butter Board, 101

brandy
  Albus Dumbledore's Apple Butter and Brandy Hot Toddy, 157
  Black Lake Cod Cakes with Poached Eggs and Brandy Cream Sauce, 92–93
  Queenie's Mini Brandied Apple Strudels with Apple Mint Sauce, 57–59

breads
  Deathly Hallows Pull-Apart Teatime Bread, 95–96
  Kowalski Bakery's Buttery Teatime Witch Hats with Magical Herbal Broomsticks, 117–119

broccoli
  Bowtruckle Island Butter Board, 101
  Butter Board, Bowtruckle Island, 101
  Butternut Squash Mini Tartlets with Crispy Bacon and Sage, Hagrid's, 107–109

centrepieces
  Queenie Goldstein's Floating Teapot, 70–73
  Champagne Cocktail, Professor Umbridge's Earl Grey Tea and Raspberry, 165

chocolate
  Chocolate Flying Keys, 139–140
  Dementors Mini Chocolate Teatime Treats, 136–137
  Divination Dream Bar Tea Treats, 24–25
  Feverless Fudge Tea Bites, 137
  Froggy Fancies, 135–136
  Goldstein Sisters' Cointreau Hot Chocolate, 160–161
  Professor Slughorn's One-Bite High Tea Profiteroles, 42–43
  Teddy the Niffler's Milk Treat, 153

cocktails
  Albus Dumbledore's Apple Butter and Brandy Hot Toddy, 157
  Ginger Witch Whisky Sour, 151
  Goldstein Sisters' Cointreau Hot Chocolate, 160–161
  The New York Ghost Wake-Up Call Drambuie Brew, 163
  Professor Umbridge's Earl Grey Tea and Raspberry Champagne Cocktail, 165
  Swooping Evil Blueberry and Mint Aviation Cocktail, 167

coffee
  The New York Ghost Wake-Up Call Drambuie Brew, 163
  Cointreau Hot Chocolate, Goldstein Sisters,' 168–169

cream, double
  Aunt Petunia's Teatime Windtorte Pudding, 23–25
  Black Lake Cod Cakes with Poached Eggs and Brandy Cream Sauce, 92–93
  Hogwarts High Table Roasted Apple Scone Bites with Fresh Cream and Mint, 18–19
  Honeydukes Lemon Drop Meringue Teatime Bites, 49–50
  Molly Weasley's Individual Teatime Rhubarb and Custard Trifles, 39–41
  The New York Ghost Wake-Up Call Drambuie Brew, 163
  Professor McGonagall's Transfigurational Sticky Toffee Pudding Bites, 37–39
  Professor Slughorn's One-Bite High Tea Profiteroles, 42–43
  Teddy the Niffler's Milk Treat, 153

cucumbers
  Durmstrang Institute Shopska Salad Tea Party Boats, 77–79

dates
  Professor McGonagall's Transfigurational Sticky Toffee Pudding Bites, 37–39
  Professor Sprouts Bite-Sized Greenhouse Mystery Cakes, 60–61
  Deathly Hallows Pull-Apart Teatime Bread, 95–96
  Dementors Mini Chocolate Teatime Treats, 136–137
  Disenchantment Tea Jellies, 133

Divination Dream Bar Tea Treats, 20–21
Dolores Umbridge's I Will Make Scones, 67

drinks. see also cocktails
  Hogwarts House Teas, 147–149
  Professor Snape's Blueberry-Sage Spritzer, 169
  Professor Trelawney's Divination Tea, 159
  Teddy the Niffler's Milk Treat, 153
  Trevor's Toad Pond Punch, 155

Dumbledore's Elderberry Tea Pastilles, 143
Durmstrang Institute Shopska Salad Tea Party Boats, 77–79

eggs
  Black Lake Cod Cakes with Poached Eggs and Brandy Cream Sauce, 92–93
  Mini Fried Raven Egg Tea Sandwiches, 79
  Pickled 'Ashwinder' Eggs, 135
  Ron Weasley's Finger Sandwiches, 83–84
  Salade Niçoise Teatime Boat Bites, 80–81
  Escargot-Stuffed Mushrooms, Ron Weasley's, 114–115
  Feverless Fudge Tea Bites, 129

fish
  Black Lake Cod Cakes with Poached Eggs and Brandy Cream Sauce, 92–93
  Salade Niçoise Teatime Boat Bites, 80–81
  Forbidden Forest Mini Mushroom Strudels, 87–89
  Froggy Fancies, 127–129
  gelatine. See jelly

gin
  Swooping Evil Blueberry and Mint Aviation Cocktail, 175
  Ginger Witch Whisky Sour, 151
  Goldstein Sisters' Cointreau Hot Chocolate, 160–161
  'Good Gravy!' Mini Meat Loaf Tea Sandwiches, 110–111
  Grandfather Goldstein's Teatime Owl Food, 139
  Great Hall Treacle and

Pinot Noir–Roasted Turkey Drumsticks, 97–98
Hagrid's Butternut Squash Mini Tartlets with Crispy Bacon and Sage, 107–109
Hagrid's Pumpkin Teatime Madeleines, 13

ham
  Aunt Petunia's Teatime Ham Bites, 110–111
  Leaky Cauldron Split Pea Teatime Soup, 85
  Ron Weasley's Finger Sandwiches, 83–84
  Hogwarts High Table Roasted Apple Scone Bites with Fresh Cream and Mint, 18–19
  Hogwarts House Teas, 147–149
  Hogwarts Houses Four-Layer Rainbow Petits Fours, 65–66

honey
  Luna Lovegood's Honey-Roasted Radish Salad, 91
  Tina Goldstein's Bite-Sized Hot Dogs with Honey Mustard Sauce, 112–113
  Honeydukes Lemon Drop Meringue Teatime Bites, 49–50
  Honeydukes Take-Home Lollipops, 149
  Hot Dogs with Honey Mustard Sauce, Tina Goldstein's Bite-Sized, 112–113
  Hungarian Horntail Mini Teatime Cakes, 26–29
  Jacob Kowalski's Mini Teatime Paczki, 17–19

jelly
  Disenchantment Tea Jellies, 133
  Dumbledore's Elderberry Tea Pastilles, 143
  Ron Weasley's Teatime Raspberry Jelly Treats, 105–106
  Kowalski Bakery's Buttery Teatime Witch Hats with Magical Herbal Broomsticks, 117–119
  Kowalski Bakery's Occamy Egg Teatime Surprise, 45–46
  Lavender Teatime Canelés, Paris Pâtisserie, 37–39
  Leaky Cauldron Split Pea Teatime Soup, 85

174

lemons
  Ginger Witch Whisky Sour, 151
  Honeydukes Lemon Drop Meringue Teatime Bites, 49–50
  Teddy the Niffler's Two-Bite Gold Coin Sandwich Cakes, 68–69
Lollipops, Honeydukes Take-Home, 149
Luna Lovegood's Honey-Roasted Radish Salad, 91
meringues
  Aunt Petunia's Teatime Windtorte Pudding, 23–25
  Honeydukes Lemon Drop Meringue Teatime Bites, 49–50
milk
  Goldstein Sisters' Cointreau Hot Chocolate, 168–169
  Teddy the Niffler's Milk Treat, 153
Mini Fried Raven Egg Tea Sandwiches, 79
mint
  Feverless Fudge Tea Bites, 137
  Hogwarts High Table Roasted Apple Scone Bites with Fresh Cream and Mint, 18–19
  The New York Ghost Wake-Up Call Drambuie Brew, 163
  Professor Slughorn's One-Bite High Tea Profiteroles, 42–43
  Queenie's Mini Brandied Apple Strudels with Apple Mint Sauce, 57–59
  Swooping Evil Blueberry and Mint Aviation Cocktail, 167
Molly Weasley's Bangers and Roasted Tomato Quiche Bites, 121–123
Molly Weasley's Individual Teatime Rhubarb and Custard Trifles, 39–41
mushrooms
  Forbidden Forest Mini Mushroom Strudels, 87–89
  Ron Weasley's Savoury Escargot-Stuffed Mushrooms, 114–115
  The New York Ghost Wake-Up Call Drambuie Brew, 163
  One-Bite Circus Animal Tea Biscuits, 53–55
oranges
  Goldstein Sisters' Cointreau Hot Chocolate, 168–169
  Place Cachée Orange-Scented Teatime Pastry Puffs, 70–71
  Professor McGonagall's Transfigurational Sticky Toffee Pudding Bites, 37–39
Paczki, Jacob Kowalski's Mini Teatime, 17–19
Paris Pâtisserie Two-Bite Lavender Teatime Canelés, 37–39
pastries
  Forbidden Forest Mini Mushroom Strudels, 87–89
  Hagrid's Butternut Squash Mini Tartlets with Crispy Bacon and Sage, 107–109
  Jacob Kowalski's Mini Teatime Paczki, 17–19
  Paris Pâtisserie Two-Bite Lavender Teatime Canelés, 37–39
  Place Cachée Orange-Scented Teatime Pastry Puffs, 70–71
  Professor Slughorn's One-Bite High Tea Profiteroles, 42–43
  Queenie's Mini Brandied Apple Strudels with Apple Mint Sauce, 57–59
  Pickled 'Ashwinder' Eggs, 135
  Place Cachée Orange-Scented Teatime Pastry Puffs, 70–71
potatoes
  Salade Niçoise Teatime Boat Bites, 80–81
  Professor McGonagall's Transfigurational Sticky Toffee Pudding Bites, 37–39
Professor Slughorn's One-Bite High Tea Profiteroles, 42–43
Professor Snape's Blueberry-Sage Spritzer, 169
Professor Sprouts Bite-sized Greenhouse Mystery Cakes, 60–61
Professor Trelawney's Divination Tea, 159
Professor Umbridge's Earl Grey Tea and Raspberry Champagne Cocktail, 165
Professor Umbridge's Load of Waffles, 31
meringues
  Aunt Petunia's Teatime Windtorte Pudding, 23–25
cakes
  Hogwarts Houses Four-Layer Rainbow Petits Fours, 65–66
  Hungarian Horntail Mini Teatime Cakes, 26–29
  Professor McGonagall's Transfigurational Sticky Toffee Pudding Bites, 37–39
  Professor Sprouts Bite-Sized Greenhouse Mystery Cakes, 60–61
  Teddy the Niffler's Two-Bite Gold Coin Sandwich Cakes, 68–69
  Pumpkin Teatime Madeleines, Hagrid's, 13
  Queenie Goldstein's Floating Teapot, 70–73
  Queenie's Mini Brandied Apple Strudels with Apple Mint Sauce, 57–59
  Quiche Bites, Molly Weasley's Bangers and Roasted Tomato, 121–123
radicchio
  Bowtruckle Island Butter Board, 101
  Salade Niçoise Teatime Boat Bites, 80–81
  Radish Salad, Luna Lovegood's Honey-Roasted, 91
raisins
  Bowtruckle Island Butter Board, 101
  Jacob Kowalski's Mini Teatime Paczki, 17–19
  Professor Sprouts Bite-Sized Greenhouse Mystery Cakes, 60–61
  Queenie's Mini Brandied Apple Strudels with Apple Mint Sauce, 57–59
raspberries
  Professor Umbridge's Earl Grey Tea and Raspberry Champagne Cocktail, 165
  Ron Weasley's Teatime Raspberry Jelly Treats, 105–106
Rhubarb and Custard Trifles, Molly Weasley's Individual Teatime, 39–41
Ron Weasley's Finger Sandwiches, 83–84
Ron Weasley's Savoury Escargot-Stuffed Mushrooms, 114–115
Ron Weasley's Teatime Raspberry Jelly Treats, 105–106
sage
  Hagrid's Butternut Squash Mini Tartlets with Crispy Bacon and Sage, 107–109
  Professor Snape's Blueberry-Sage Spritzer, 169
  Salade Niçoise Teatime Boat Bites, 80–81
salads
  Durmstrang Institute Shopska Salad Tea Party Boats, 77–79
  Luna Lovegood's Honey-Roasted Radish Salad, 91
  Ron Weasley's Teatime Raspberry Jelly Treats, 105–106
  Salade Niçoise Teatime Boat Bites, 80–81
sandwiches
  'Good Gravy!' Mini Meat Loaf Tea Sandwiches, 110–111
  Mini Fried Raven Egg Tea Sandwiches, 79
  Ron Weasley's Finger Sandwiches, 83–84
  Teddy the Niffler's Two-Bite Gold Coin Sandwich Cakes, 68–69
sausage
  Molly Weasley's Bangers and Roasted Tomato Quiche Bites, 121–123
scones
  Dolores Umbridge's I Will Make Scones, 67
  Hogwarts High Table Roasted Apple Scone Bites with Fresh Cream and Mint, 18–19
  Split Pea Teatime Soup, Leaky Cauldron, 85
sweets
  Disenchantment Tea Jellies, 133
  Dumbledore's Elderberry Tea Pastilles, 143
  Swooping Evil Blueberry and Mint Aviation Cocktail, 167
tea
  Hogwarts House Teas, 147–149
  Hogwarts Houses Four-Layer Rainbow Petits Fours, 65–66
  Professor Trelawney's Divination Tea, 159
  Professor Umbridge's Earl Grey Tea and Raspberry Champagne Cocktail, 165
  Teddy the Niffler's Milk Treat, 153
  Teddy the Niffler's Two-Bite Gold Coin Sandwich Cakes, 68–69
  Tina Goldstein's Bite-Sized Hot Dogs with Honey Mustard Sauce, 112–113
Toffee Pudding Bites, Sticky, Professor McGonagall's Transfigurational, 37–39
tomatoes
  Deathly Hallows Pull-Apart Teatime Bread, 95–96
  Durmstrang Institute Shopska Salad Tea Party Boats, 77–79
  Molly Weasley's Bangers and Roasted Tomato Quiche Bites, 121–123
  Professor Sprouts Bite-Sized Greenhouse Mystery Cakes, 60–61
  Ron Weasley's Finger Sandwiches, 83–84
  Salade Niçoise Teatime Boat Bites, 80–81
Treacle and Pinot Noir–Roasted Turkey Drumsticks, Great Hall, 97–98
Trevor's Toad Pond Punch, 155
Trifles, Molly Weasley's Individual Teatime Rhubarb and Custard, 39–41
Turkey Drumsticks, Treacle and Pinot Noir–Roasted, Great Hall, 97–98
Waffles, Professor Umbridge's Load of, 31
walnuts
  Divination Dream Bar Tea Treats, 20–21
  Grandfather Goldstein's Teatime Owl Food, 131
  Professor Sprouts Bite-Sized Greenhouse Mystery Cakes, 60–61
whisky
  Aunt Petunia's Teatime Ham Bites, 110–111
  Ginger Witch Whisky Sour, 151
  The New York Ghost Wake-Up Call Drambuie Brew, 163
  Professor McGonagall's Transfigurational Sticky Toffee Pudding Bites, 37–39
white chocolate
  Kowalski Bakery's Occamy Egg Teatime Surprise, 45–46
wine
  Great Hall Treacle and Pinot Noir–Roasted Turkey Drumsticks, 97–98

175

First published in Great Britain in 2024 by

Greenfinch
An imprint of Quercus Editions Ltd
Carmelite House
50 Victoria Embankment
London EC4Y 0DZ
An Hachette UK company

Copyright © 2024 Warner Bros. Entertainment Inc. WIZARDING WORLD characters, names and related indicia are © & ™ Warner Bros. Entertainment Inc. WB SHIELD: © & ™ WBEI. Publishing Rights © JKR. (s24)

All rights reserved. Published in the US by Insight Editions, San Rafael, California, in 2024.
No part of this book may be reproduced in any form without written permission from the publisher.

ISBN: 978-1-52943-499-6

Photographer: Ted Thomas
Food and Prop Stylist: Elena P. Craig
Assistant Food Stylist: Patricia Parrish
Photoshoot Art Director: Judy Wiatrek Trum
Illustrations: Paula Hanback

Insight Editions, in association with Roots of Peace, will plant two trees for each tree used in the manufacturing of this book. Roots of Peace is an internationally renowned humanitarian organization dedicated to eradicating land mines worldwide and converting war-torn lands into productive farms and wildlife habitats. Roots of Peace will plant two million fruit and nut trees in Afghanistan and provide farmers there with the skills and support necessary for sustainable land use.

Manufactured in China by Insight Editions

10 9 8 7 6 5 4 3 2 1

CONCEPT ART

Page 8

Ron and Harry arrive at the Weasley home, The Burrow, via a flying car in *Harry Potter and the Chamber of Secrets* in artwork by Andrew Williamson.

Page 29

Concept art by Paul Catling of the Hungarian Horntail, Harry's dragon for the Triwizard Tournament's first task in *Harry Potter and the Goblet of Fire*.

Page 167

Studies of the Swooping Evil by artist Dan Baker for *Fantastic Beasts and Where to Find Them* explored the terrifying creature in its cocoon form and with its wings fully open.